Note for parents

Using a dictionary requires several different skills, from identifying the letters in a word to recognizing the order of letters in the alphabet. This picture dictionary is designed to help your child develop these key abilities. Answers for all the activities are on page 128.

To help your child get the most benefit from this picture dictionary, the following suggestions may be useful:

⭐ To help your child to find a particular word in the dictionary, point to the alphabet strip on each page and encourage your child to look for the initial letter of the word they need. Ask them to find the page(s) with that letter highlighted.

⭐ Once on the page, your child may need support to find the word they are looking for. Help them to use the alphabet strip to work out where the second, third etc. letters in the word fall in the alphabet, then look through the word lists to locate it.

⭐ The pictures are designed to give clues to help your child predict the word and its meaning, so it may be useful to look at the pictures first.

⭐ Use the gold stars as incentives and rewards for your child learning some of the words or spellings on each page.

This edition published by Parragon Books Ltd in 2016

Parragon Books Ltd
Chartist House
15–17 Trim Street
Bath BA1 1HA, UK
www.parragon.com

Copyright © Parragon Books Ltd 2016

Illustrated by Simon Abbott

ISBN 978-1-4748-4742-1
Printed in China

My First
Picture
Dictionary

Bath · New York · Cologne · Melbourne · Delhi
Hong Kong · Shenzhen · Singapore

Wonderful words

Welcome to the wonderful world of words! There are some useful things to know before you use this dictionary…

⭐ A dictionary is a book of words and their meanings, in alphabetical order.

⭐ It is easy to use a dictionary if you know your alphabet.

⭐ You can use a dictionary to learn a new word, to learn to spell a word, and to learn what a word means.

⭐ There are 26 letters in the alphabet.

⭐ Letters are put together to make words. We use words to make sentences.

Did you know?

In English, the letter 'e' is used more than any other letter.

More words start with the letter 's' than any other letter.

Words that rhyme have the same sound. The words sing, bring, sting and thing all rhyme.

There is no word that rhymes with 'orange'.

You can remember how to spell '–ight' words, such as light, night and fight, with this simple phrase: **I**'ve **G**ot **H**airy **T**oes!

Use the dictionary to help you find the answers to these questions about the alphabet:

What letter comes before 'F'?

What letter comes after 'S'?

Words about words

Noun

A noun is a word that names something (such as a person, animal, place, object or feeling). Nouns are also called naming words. These words are nouns: mother, Tom, teacher, elephant, dog, school, garden, ball, computer.

Adjective

A word that describes a noun. Adjectives are sometimes called describing words. These words are adjectives: delicious, cold, noisy, green, small, heavy, happy, clever.

Verb

A verb describes an action. Verbs are sometimes called doing words. These words are verbs: count, sing, jump, run, argue, write.

Adverb

A word that describes a verb, adjective or another adverb. These words are adverbs: quickly, happily, here, downstairs, now, early.

Preposition

A word that describes a noun compared to another word. These words are prepositions: on, under, above, after, before.

Use the dictionary to find out if these words are nouns or verbs.

helicopter   **fall**   **cave**

sniff   **magazine**   **write**

atlas   **sock**   **melon**

Clue: look next to the headwords!

Can you find...

2 nouns in the dictionary?

2 verbs in the dictionary?

2 adjectives in the dictionary?

Lots of letters

All words are made up of letters. Each letter has a name and a sound. Say each of these sentences aloud to hear the sound that each letter makes.

Aa is for apple	**Nn** is for nest
Bb is for banana	**Oo** is for orange
Cc is for cake	**Pp** is for pizza
Dd is for dog	**Qq** is for queen
Ee is for elephant	**Rr** is for rabbit
Ff is for fairy	**Ss** is for sandcastle
Gg is for gate	**Tt** is for teddy bear
Hh is for hat	**Uu** is for umbrella
Ii is for igloo	**Vv** is for vegetable
Jj is for jar	**Ww** is for wood
Kk is for kite	**Xx** is for axe
Ll is for lemon	**Yy** is for yo-yo
Mm is for moon	**Zz** is for zebra

Using the dictionary

There are five parts to each entry in the dictionary. Use the guide below to help you read each entry and find the information you need.

The type of word
This tells you if the word is a noun, adjective, verb or adverb.

The headword
These will be in alphabetical order.

The definition
This explains the meaning of the word.

apple (noun)
An apple is a round and crunchy fruit. Apples grow on trees.

Apples can be red or green.

The example sentence
This shows how you could use the word in a complete sentence.

The picture
This will help you to guess what the word means.

Aa

above (preposition)
Something is above when it is higher than something else.

The bird flies above the clouds.

acrobat (noun)
An acrobat is someone who can do exciting gymnastic tricks.

The acrobat walked along a tightrope.

accident (noun)
An accident is something that happens by mistake.

The boy had an accident on his bicycle.

add (verb)
When you add, you put two or more numbers together to make a bigger number.

If you add the numbers 7 and 3, the answer is 10.

$7 + 3 = 10$ ✓

acorn (noun)
An acorn is a type of nut. Acorns grow on oak trees.

Acorns fall to the ground.

address (noun)
Your address is the name or number of your house, your street, town or city and your postcode.

The girl wrote the address on the envelope.

adult (noun)
An adult is a person or animal that is grown-up.

Parents and grandparents are adults.

air (noun)
Air is all around us. We breathe air to stay alive.

You breathe air in and out of your nose and mouth.

aeroplane (noun)
An aeroplane is a machine with wings. It flies in the sky.

People travel in aeroplanes to get to different parts of the world.

airport (noun)
An airport is the place where aeroplanes take off and land.

You go to an airport before you get on an aeroplane.

afraid (adjective)
When you are afraid, you feel that something bad might happen.

My cat is afraid of the big dog next door.

alarm (noun)
An alarm is a sound or sign that warns you about something.

The fire alarm rang loudly.

afternoon (noun)
The afternoon is the time between morning and evening.

The children played in the park in the afternoon.

alien (noun)
An alien is a made-up creature from another planet.

The alien travelled to Earth in a flying saucer.

11

a
b
c
d
e
f
g
h
i
j
k
l
m
n
o
p
q
r
s
t
u
v
w
x
y
z

alligator (noun)

An alligator is an animal with scaly skin, long jaws and sharp teeth. It looks like a crocodile.

Alligators use their long tails to swim.

ankle (noun)

Your ankle is the part of your body where your leg joins your foot.

Your ankle feels bony.

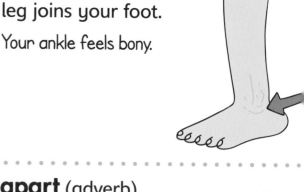

ambulance (noun)

An ambulance is a vehicle that takes sick or injured people to hospital.

An ambulance has flashing lights and a siren.

apart (adverb)

Two things are apart if they are away from each other.

The singer was standing with her feet apart.

angry (adjective)

If you are feeling angry, you are annoyed or in a bad mood.

The giant was angry because Jack had taken his gold.

app (noun)

App is short for application. A computer application lets you do things, like work or play a game.

You can use an app on a phone to play games.

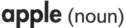

animal (noun)

An animal is something that is alive. Animals move, eat, grow and have children.

Monkeys, parrots, snakes and people are animals.

apple (noun)

An apple is a round and crunchy fruit. Apples grow on trees.

Apples can be red or green.

argue (verb)

You argue with someone when you want or feel different things.

My big sisters always argue with each other.

astronaut (noun)

An astronaut is someone who travels into outer space.

Astronauts have walked on the moon.

arm (noun)

Your arm is the part of your body between your shoulder and your hand.

Most people have two arms.

athlete (noun)

An athlete is someone who is good at sports such as running, jumping and throwing.

The athlete took part in a high jump competition.

artist (noun)

An artist is someone who draws or paints pictures.

The artist used paints to make art.

atlas (noun)

An atlas is a book of maps. It shows where countries and towns are.

We used my atlas to see where we were going on holiday.

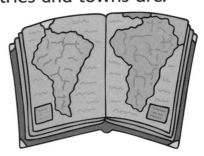

asleep (adjective)

You are asleep when you are not awake. When you are asleep your body and mind are resting.

Your eyes are closed when you are asleep.

awake (adjective)

You are awake when you are not asleep. You know what is going on around you.

Your eyes are open when you are awake.

Bb

baby (noun)

A baby is a very young child. Babies cannot walk or talk.

A baby drinks milk because it can't eat solid food yet.

badge (noun)

A badge is a small piece of metal, plastic or cloth that you stick onto something.

I have a badge on my football shirt.

bag (noun)

You use a bag to hold and carry things. Bags for carrying food are usually made of paper or plastic.

We carried our shopping home in bags.

bake (verb)

When you bake something, you cook it in a hot, dry oven.

Grandpa bakes delicious cakes.

balance (verb)

If you balance, you keep yourself steady.

The acrobat balanced on one leg.

ball (noun)

A ball is a round object that you can throw, kick or hit in a game.

A beach ball is brightly coloured.

ballet (noun)

Ballet is a type of dance that tells a story through actions and music.

I went to a ballet class.

bark (noun)

Bark is the hard, outside part of a tree. It covers the tree's trunk, branches and twigs.

The bark of most trees has an interesting pattern.

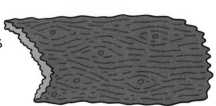

balloon (noun)

A balloon is a shaped rubber bag that you fill up with air and tie at one end.

I had red balloons at my party.

bark (verb)

When an animal barks, it makes a loud noise.

Our dog barks at the postman.

banana (noun)

A banana is a long fruit with a yellow skin. Bananas only grow in hot countries.

Peel off the banana skin before you eat the fruit.

barn (noun)

A barn is a big building on a farm. A farmer keeps animals or supplies inside a barn.

In winter, cows live in a barn to keep warm.

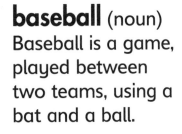

bandage (noun)

A bandage is a strip of cloth. You put a bandage around a part of your body that is hurt.

I've got a small bandage because I hurt my finger.

baseball (noun)

Baseball is a game, played between two teams, using a bat and a ball.

In baseball, you hit the ball with a long bat.

basket (noun)
You use a basket to hold and carry things. Baskets are usually made of metal or wood.

We use a basket when we go to the shops.

beak (noun)
The hard part of a bird's mouth is called a beak. A bird uses its beak to pick up food.

The parrot's beak is yellow.

bathroom (noun)
A bathroom is the room where you wash.

We have a basin, a toilet, a bath and a shower in our bathroom.

bean (noun)
Beans are the seeds of some plants. They are a vegetable. Beans often grow in pods.

You can take beans out of their pods before you cook them.

beach (noun)
A beach is the land next to a lake or the sea. Beaches are covered in sand or small stones.

We stand on the beach to watch the dolphins leap in and out of the sea.

bear (noun)
A bear is a large wild animal. Bears have thick fur, a short tail and long claws.

A bear looks tall when it stands on its back legs.

bead (noun)
A bead is a small piece of glass, wood or plastic that has a hole through the middle.

You can put coloured beads onto a string to make a necklace.

beard (noun)
A beard is the hair that grows on a man's chin and cheeks.

My dad's beard tickles my face when he kisses me.

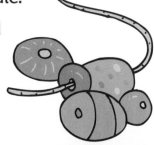

beautiful (adjective)

Beautiful means lovely to look at or listen to.

The sky looks beautiful at sunset.

bell (noun)

A bell is a hollow metal object that makes a noise when you hit it. It often has a small piece of metal inside, which makes a noise when you shake the bell.

The bells in our school make a loud noise.

become (verb)

To become is to grow to be something different.

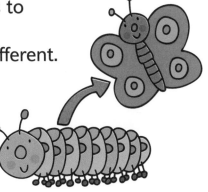

A caterpillar becomes a butterfly.

below (preposition)

Something is below when it is lower than something else.

The mole lives below the ground.

bee (noun)

A bee is a flying insect with six legs. Some bees make honey and live in a hive.

Bees visit colourful flowers in the garden.

belt (noun)

A belt is a long piece of leather or plastic that you wear around your waist to hold your clothes in place.

My belt stops my trousers from falling down.

believe (verb)

To believe is to feel certain that something is true.

Do you believe in the tooth fairy?

bench (noun)

A bench is a long seat. It is usually made of wood, metal or stone.

The old lady sits on the park bench.

17

a
b
c
d
e
f
g
h
i
j
k
l
m
n
o
p
q
r
s
t
u
v
w
x
y
z

bend (verb)

To bend means to make something become more curved or angled.

If you want to touch your toes, you must bend your body.

birthday (noun)

Your birthday is a day to celebrate the day you were born. Your birthday is on the same date every year.

Today is my birthday!

bicycle (noun)

A bicycle is a vehicle that has two wheels that go round when you push on the pedals.

My new bicycle is bright red.

bite (verb)

To bite means to take hold of something, or cut into something, with your teeth.

You bite an apple and then you chew.

binoculars (noun)

When you look through binoculars, things that are far away look closer.

My uncle uses binoculars to watch birds flying in the sky.

blackberry (noun)

A blackberry is a soft, juicy fruit. Blackberries grow on bushes and in hedges.

We picked lots of blackberries to make a pie.

bird (noun)

A bird is an animal with feathers, wings and a beak. Birds lay eggs.

Birds will visit your garden if you put food out for them.

blanket (noun)

A blanket is a large piece of material, usually made of wool or soft cloth.

I like to snuggle under my blanket.

blizzard (noun)

A blizzard is when a lot of snow falls and there are also strong winds.

There was a blizzard warning on the news.

body (noun)

Your body is every part of you, from your head to your toes.

To keep my body healthy, I exercise and eat good food.

blood (noun)

Blood is the red liquid inside your body. It carries oxygen around your body.

When I accidentally cut my finger, blood came out.

boil (verb)

When a liquid boils, it bubbles and turns into steam. It will be very hot.

You can see bubbles on the top of boiling water.

blow (verb)

To blow is to move air one way.

Blow out the candle on your birthday cake!

bone (noun)

Bones are the hard parts inside your body. All the bones in your body make up your skeleton.

You have more than 200 bones in your body.

boat (noun)

A boat is a vehicle used to travel across water. Most boats have oars, sails or an engine to make them move.

The Owl and the Pussycat went to sea in a beautiful pea-green boat.

bonfire (noun)

A bonfire is a large, open fire that adults make outdoors. It is dangerous to stand close to a fire.

Dad burns sticks and leaves on a bonfire.

a b c d e f g h i j k l m n o p q r s t u v w x y z

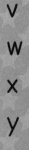

book (noun)

A book is an object made of pieces of paper that are joined together.

A storybook has words and pictures in it.

box (noun)

A box is a container with sides and a flat base. It usually has a lid. It can be made from cardboard, plastic, wood or metal.

Do you keep your toys inside a box?

borrow (verb)

To borrow means to take and use something that belongs to someone else. After you have borrowed something, you give it back.

You can borrow my pencil.

boy (noun)

A boy is a male child. When a boy grows up, he becomes a man.

The boy is much smaller than his dad.

bottle (noun)

A bottle is an object with empty space inside, used for holding liquids. Most bottles are made of glass or plastic.

There are lots of bottles in my kitchen.

brain (noun)

Your brain is inside your head. You use your brain to think and feel.

Your brain helps you to remember things.

bounce (verb)

When something bounces, it moves quickly in a different direction after hitting something hard.

The ball bounced off the wall.

branch (noun)

A branch is the part of a tree that grows outwards from the trunk.

A rope ladder hangs from the branch of the tree.

20

brave (adjective)

If you are brave, you are ready to do or face something even when it is scary or hard.

The brave children got to the top of the climbing wall.

breathe (verb)

When you breathe, you take air into your body and then let it out again.

You breathe through your nose and mouth.

bread (noun)

Bread is a food made mainly from flour and water. You bake bread in an oven.

You can make toast with a slice of bread.

brick (noun)

A brick is a small block made of hard clay. You use bricks to build things.

We use bricks like these to build houses.

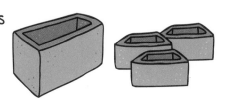

break (verb)

If you break something, it goes into smaller pieces.

Did you break the window?

bridge (noun)

A bridge is a structure that goes over something so that people can cross.

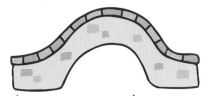

Most bridges go over roads, railways or rivers.

breakfast (noun)

Breakfast is the first meal you have each day. You eat it in the morning.

I like to eat cereal for my breakfast.

bright (adjective)

If something is bright, it is a strong colour. Something bright is not dull.

My jumper is bright red.

bring (verb)
To bring means to take someone, or something, to a place.

"Please bring your book to school," said the teacher.

bubble (noun)
A bubble is a ball made of liquid, with gas inside.

There are bubbles in soapy water.

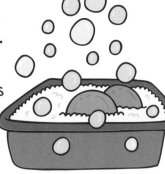

broad (adjective)
Broad means very wide. If something is broad, it is a long way from one side to the other side.

It took a long time to cross the broad river.

bucket (noun)
A bucket is an open container with a handle used to hold and carry things.

I filled the bucket with cold water.

broom (noun)
A broom is a brush with a long handle. You use a broom to sweep the floor or the ground.

He sweeps up leaves with a broom.

buckle (noun)
A buckle joins two ends of a belt or strap together.

There is a buckle on this belt.

brother (noun)
Your brother is a boy or a man with the same parents as you.

My brother is younger than me.

build (verb)
To build something is to put lots of different parts together to make something else.

My uncle is building a brick wall.

22

bulldozer (noun)

A bulldozer is a big vehicle that moves heavy stones and soil to clear the ground.

This bulldozer is working on a building site.

butter (noun)

Butter is a yellow food that is made from cow's milk. You can spread it on bread, or cook with it.

The butter is on a blue plate.

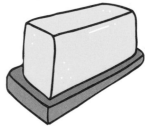

bus (noun)

A bus is a large vehicle that carries many people from place to place.

Do you go to school by bus?

butterfly (noun)

A butterfly is a flying insect with four large, colourful wings.

A butterfly spreads its wings to warm up in the sunshine.

bush (noun)

A bush is a large plant that has lots of stems growing close to the ground.

Roses grow on a rose bush.

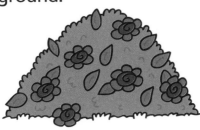

button (noun)

A button is a small circle of wood or plastic that can be sewn onto clothes. You use a button to hold two pieces of material together.

There is a green and blue button on my top.

busy (adjective)

A person who is busy has lots of things to do.

My aunt is busy at work all day.

buy (verb)

To buy means to give money and get something in return.

I went to the shops to buy some new clothes.

23

a b c d e f g h i j k l m n o p q r s t u v w x y z

Cc

cactus (noun)
A cactus is a prickly plant with a thick stem. It grows in hot, dry places.

This cactus has bright red flowers.

calf (noun)
A calf is a baby cow, a baby elephant, a baby rhinoceros or a baby whale.

The calf is standing with its mother.

cake (noun)
Cake is a soft, sweet food, often made from flour, sugar, eggs and butter. You bake a cake in an oven.

I had a cake on my birthday.

camel (noun)
A camel is a large, long-necked animal with one or two humps on its back. Camels live in dry places.

I saw a camel when I went on holiday.

calculator (noun)
A calculator is a machine with a keyboard of numbers. It can do sums quickly.

You can use a calculator to check your maths.

camera (noun)
A camera can record photographs and videos. Most mobile phones now work as cameras too.

Do you take a camera with you when you go on holiday?

canal (noun)
A canal is a type of river made by people. It is usually straight.

Special narrowboats travel along canals.

cardboard (noun)
Cardboard is a thick paper. It does not bend as easily as other types of paper.

Cereal boxes are made from cardboard.

candle (noun)
A candle is a block of wax with a piece of string in the middle. When you burn the string, it gives you light.

The wax on this candle is starting to melt.

carrot (noun)
A carrot is an orange vegetable. It grows under the ground.

Carrots are my favourite vegetable.

canoe (noun)
A canoe is a narrow boat with pointed ends. You use a paddle to move a canoe through water.

My brother and I paddled our canoe.

carry (verb)
To carry is to move something from one place to another.

My teacher asked me to carry a pile of books.

cape (noun)
A cape is a coat with no sleeves.

Witches and wizards wear capes.

cartoon (noun)
A cartoon is a funny drawing or lots of funny drawings which tell a story.

We watch cartoons on the television.

25

a b c d e f g h i j k l m n o p q r s t u v w x y z

a
b
c
d
e
f
g
h
i
j
k
l
m
n
o
p
q
r
s
t
u
v
w
x
y
z

case (noun)
A case is a container that you can keep things in. You can use a case to carry things around.

I keep my colouring pencils in a pencil case.

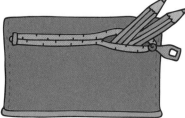

caterpillar (noun)
A caterpillar is a young insect. When it is older, a caterpillar becomes a butterfly.

Caterpillars have lots of legs.

castle (noun)
A castle is a big building with thick walls. Most castles were built a long time ago.

This castle was built on top of a hill.

cave (noun)
A cave is a large space underground, usually in the side of a hill or cliff.

This cave has water in it.

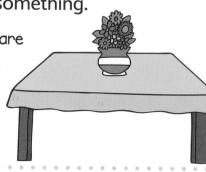

cat (noun)
A cat is a small pet animal with soft fur, four legs and a long tail.

My cat has orange fur.

centre (noun)
The centre is the very middle of something.

The flowers are in the centre of the table.

catch (verb)
To catch is to take hold of something when it is moving. You usually catch with your hands.

The goalkeeper caught the ball.

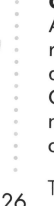

chain (noun)
A chain is a long row of rings that are joined together. Chains are usually made of metal or plastic.

The chain is grey.

26

chair (noun)

A chair is something that you sit on. Most chairs have four legs and a back.

My mum's chair is blue.

chase (verb)

To chase means to try to catch someone or something.

Our dog likes to chase cats.

chalk (noun)

A chalk is a stick of soft rock. You use chalk to write on a chalkboard.

There are many different colours of chalk in this box.

cheap (adjective)

If something is cheap, it is sold for a low price.

The bananas in this market are cheap.

change (verb)

To change means to make something different.

My little sister changes her clothes after school.

cheese (noun)

Cheese is a food made from milk. It can be hard or soft. Some cheeses smell strong.

The small piece of cheese has holes in it.

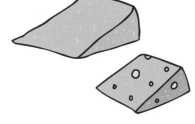

change (noun)

When you pay too much money for something, the money you get back is called change.

I bought an ice cream and the man gave me some change.

cherry (noun)

A cherry is a small, round fruit. It is usually bright or dark red. A cherry has a hard stone in the middle.

These cherries come in a pair.

chick (noun)
A chick is any kind of baby bird.

There are four fluffy chicks in this nest.

chocolate (noun)
Chocolate is a sweet food. It is made from cocoa and sugar.

Chocolate often comes in wrapped bars like this one.

chicken (noun)
A chicken is a farm bird. A female chicken is called a hen, and a male chicken is called a cockerel.

A female chicken lays eggs.

choose (verb)
To choose means to pick between more than one option.

I take a long time to choose which shirt to wear.

child (noun)
A child is a young person. Children have not grown up.

The child held his mum's hand.

circus (noun)
A circus is a show with clowns and acrobats, usually in a large tent.

You watch a circus inside a big tent.

chimpanzee (noun)
A chimpanzee is a wild animal with long arms and no tail. Chimpanzees live in Africa.

The chimpanzee swings in the tree.

city (noun)
A city is a big town.

There are lots of buildings in a city.

28

clap (verb)

To clap is to hit your hands together to make a noise.

My baby sister can clap her hands.

cliff (noun)

A cliff is a tall hill near the sea. Most cliffs are made of rock.

There is a cliff next to the beach.

class (noun)

A class is a group of children who learn together.

There are six children in my dance class.

climb (verb)

When you climb, you go up something. You usually use your hands and feet to climb.

My brother likes to climb on the climbing frame.

claw (noun)

A claw is the hard, sharp nail at the end of an animal's finger or toe.

This monster has long claws.

clock (noun)

A clock is a machine that shows you what time it is. It shows hours and minutes, and sometimes seconds.

An alarm clock makes a loud noise to wake you up.

clean (adjective)

When something is clean, there is no dirt or mess on it. Clean is the opposite of dirty.

I make sure my hands are clean before cooking.

clothes (noun)

Clothes are the things you wear to cover your body.

Skirts, shorts and T-shirts are clothes.

29

a
b
c
d
e
f
g
h
i
j
k
l
m
n
o
p
q
r
s
t
u
v
w
x
y
z

cloud (noun)

A cloud is a patch of tiny water droplets floating in the sky. Clouds are white, grey or black.

Rain comes from clouds.

coin (noun)

A coin is a small, flat piece of metal. Coins are used as money.

This coin has a picture of a bird on it.

clown (noun)

A clown is a person who dresses up and does funny tricks. A clown usually performs in a circus.

Clowns do silly things to make people laugh.

cold (adjective)

When something is cold, it is not hot. When there is snow it feels very cold.

Do you get cold when you build a snowman?

coat (noun)

A coat is a piece of clothing you wear on top of your clothes when you go outside.

My coat keeps me warm when it is cold.

cold (noun)

If you have a cold, you are not well. You usually have a runny nose, a sore throat and you sneeze a lot. I sneeze and cough when I have a cold.

coconut (noun)

A coconut is a big, brown seed with a hard shell. It grows on tall trees in hot countries.

The outside of a coconut is covered in brown hair.

30

colour (noun)

A colour is the way that something looks in daylight. Red, blue and green are colours.

My paint box has eight colours in it.

comb (noun)

A comb is a piece of plastic, wood or metal with a row of thin spikes. You use it to keep your hair tidy.

The spikes on a comb are called teeth.

cook (verb)

To cook means to prepare food by chopping, mixing or heating it up.

I like it when we cook at school.

compass (noun)

A compass is an object used to show where you are going. The arrow points to the north.

An explorer uses a compass.

cottage (noun)

A cottage is a small house. Most cottages are in the countryside.

This cottage has a roof made of straw.

computer (noun)

A computer is a machine that stores and sorts information and allows you to access the Internet.

I keep music and photos on my computer.

count (verb)

To count is to say numbers in order, or to find out how many things there are in total.

I counted five ducks on the pond.

container (noun)

A container is an object that is used for holding or moving something.

The cakes are in the plastic container.

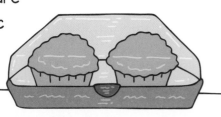

cow (noun)

A cow is a female farm animal. Cows can make milk.

This cow is called Buttercup.

31

a b c d e f g h i j k l m n o p q r s t u v w x y z

crab (noun)
A crab is an animal with a hard shell. It has two claws and eight legs.

Have you ever seen a crab on the beach?

crayon (noun)
A crayon is a stick made of coloured wax. You use a crayon to draw a picture.

I drew a tree with my green crayon.

crane (noun)
A crane is a large, tall machine with a long arm. It can lift and move heavy things.

The crane is lifting a very heavy pipe.

crocodile (noun)
A crocodile is a large reptile with scaly skin, long jaws and sharp teeth. It looks like an alligator.

Crocodiles swim in rivers in some hot countries.

crash (verb)
To crash is to bump into something.

I don't want to crash my bike.

crooked (adjective)
Crooked means bent or twisted out of place.

The old man had a crooked stick.

crawl (verb)
To crawl is to move along close to the ground, using your hands and knees.

Most babies crawl before they can walk.

crowd (noun)
A crowd is a lot of people together in the same place.

There was a crowd of parents at the school gate.

crown (noun)
A crown is a ring of metal worn on your head. Kings and queens wear crowns.

The gold crown was decorated with jewels.

cup (noun)
A cup is a small bowl with a handle. You can put a drink into a cup.

My mum's favourite cup has a matching saucer.

cry (verb)
To cry is to make tears. You cry when you are hurt, or when you feel sad.

I cried when my toy car broke.

cupboard (noun)
A cupboard is a piece of furniture that you keep things in. It has a door on the front and often has shelves inside. We keep our saucepans in a cupboard.

cucumber (noun)
A cucumber is a long, thin fruit. It has green skin, and it is soft inside.

I eat slices of cucumber as a snack.

curtain (noun)
A curtain is a piece of material that hangs by a window. You pull the curtain across the window to cover it.

My bedroom curtains have rockets and stars on them.

cuddle (verb)
When you cuddle someone, or something, you put your arms around them and hold them close.

I cuddle my teddy at night.

cut (verb)
When you cut something, you open or divide it. You can use a knife or scissors to cut.

We cut the pizza into six slices.

Dd

daisy (noun)

A daisy is a small flower with white or pink petals and a yellow centre.

Daisies grow in our garden.

dark (adjective)

Dark means little or no light. When it is dark, you cannot see clearly.

You use a torch at night because it is dark outside.

dance (verb)

To dance is to move about in time to music.

I love to dance with my friends.

day (noun)

A day starts at midnight and is 24 hours long. There are usually 365 days in each year.

There are seven days in one week.

danger (noun)

Danger means that something bad might happen. If there is danger, you may get hurt. The fishing boat was in danger at sea.

decorate (verb)

To decorate something means to add things to change how it looks.

We decorate our front door with balloons and streamers before a party.

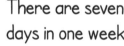

34

deep (adjective)
If something is deep, it goes down a long way from the top.

I can dive into the swimming pool at the deep end.

dessert (noun)
A dessert is a sweet food that you eat at the end of a meal.

Today my dessert has pink cream and a cherry on top.

deer (noun)
A deer is a wild animal that can run fast. Most deer live near trees.

A male deer has big antlers.

diamond (noun)
A diamond is a hard stone that sparkles. Most diamonds are clear, like glass.

The gold ring has a large diamond in it.

dentist (noun)
A dentist is a person who helps you to keep your teeth clean and healthy.

I sit in a big chair when I visit the dentist.

dice (noun)
Dice are cubes. They each have six sides with a different number of dots on each side, from one to six.

We often throw dice when we play a board game.

desert (noun)
A desert is a very dry place. Few plants and animals live in deserts. Most deserts are hot places.

This desert is kept hot by the sun.

dig (verb)
To dig is to make a hole in soil or sand. You can use a spade, a machine or your hands to dig.

My dog used her paws to dig in the garden.

35

a b c d e f g h i j k l m n o p q r s t u v w x y z

a
b
c
d
e
f
g
h
i
j
k
l
m
n
o
p
q
r
s
t
u
v
w
x
y
z

dinosaur (noun)

A dinosaur is an animal that lived a very long time ago. There are no dinosaurs alive today.

Some dinosaurs were as tall as trees.

doctor (noun)

A doctor is a person who takes care of you when you are ill or hurt. Doctors try to make people better.

This doctor looks after people in hospital.

dirty (adjective)

When something is dirty, it is covered in something else. Dirty is the opposite of clean. My shoes are dirty because they're covered in mud.

dog (noun)

A dog is a furry animal with four legs. Dogs are often kept as pets.

This dog is white with black spots.

diver (noun)

A diver is a person who goes under water. A diver wears a special suit to keep warm.

The diver found a crab at the bottom of the sea.

dolphin (noun)

A dolphin is an animal that lives in the sea. Dolphins are clever and are often friendly.

Lots of dolphins swim together.

divide (verb)

To divide means to split something into smaller parts.

Mum divided the flowers into two bunches.

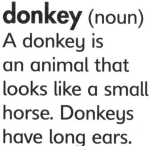

donkey (noun)

A donkey is an animal that looks like a small horse. Donkeys have long ears.

There is a donkey on my aunt's farm.

dove (noun)

A dove is a kind of bird with a small head, short legs and a plump body. They are often used as a symbol of peace.

A dove makes a quiet "coo, coo" noise.

drink (verb)

To drink means to put liquid into your mouth and swallow it.

I love to drink orange juice.

download (verb)

If you download something, you copy it from one computer system to your own computer, phone or music player.

I am going to download some music from the Internet.

drive (verb)

To drive is to make a vehicle go where you want it to go.

My uncle drives a green lorry.

dragon (noun)

A dragon is a made-up creature that flies and breathes out fire.

I like to read about dragons in storybooks.

drum (noun)

A drum is a musical instrument. You hit a drum to make a sound.

When I play my drum, I make lots of noise.

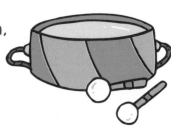

draw (verb)

To draw, you make a picture or a pattern on paper or another surface.

My brother can draw really well.

duck (noun)

A duck is a kind of bird that has a flat beak, a large body and webbed feet to help it swim.

I like to feed the ducks in the park.

Ee

eagle (noun)

An eagle is a large bird with long, broad wings. Eagles hunt mice and rabbits.

An eagle's sharp claws are called talons.

eat (verb)

When you eat, you put food in your mouth, chew it, and then swallow it.

My sister loves to eat spaghetti.

ear (noun)

Ears are the part of your body that you hear with. You have two ears.

I listen to music with my ears.

egg (noun)

Eggs are the objects laid by birds, reptiles, insects and fish. An egg usually has a hard shell and a baby animal grows inside it.

A baby chick has to break out of its egg.

early (adjective)

If you are early, you arrive before the expected time. Early means not late.

When I get to school early, I wait outside the gate.

elbow (noun)

An elbow is the hard, bony part of your arm where your arm bends.

You have to bend your elbows when you lift something heavy.

38

electricity (noun)

Electricity is a kind of energy. It makes many machines work by giving them power.

Electricity comes into our homes along wires.

envelope (noun)

An envelope is a flat paper container for a letter. You put a letter inside an envelope.

I use envelopes when I send letters to my friends.

elephant (noun)

An elephant is a large, wild animal. It has big ears and its long nose is called a trunk.

The elephant is the biggest animal that lives on land.

equal (adjective)

Equal means being the same number, or the same size.

You have an equal number of fingers on each hand.

email (noun)

An email is a message sent from one computer to another. Email is short for 'electronic mail'.

I will send an email to my uncle, to thank him for my present.

evening (noun)

The evening is the end of the daytime and the start of the night. It comes after the afternoon.

The sun goes down in the evening, and the sky turns dark.

enter (verb)

To enter means to go into a place. You enter a room through a door.

When I enter the toyshop, I see lots of toys.

eye (noun)

You have two eyes on your face. You see with your eyes.

My sister has blue eyes.

Ff

face (noun)
Your face is the front part of your head. Your eyes, nose and mouth are all on your face.

Can you make a funny face?

family (noun)
A family is a group of people who are related.

There are four people in my family.

fairy (noun)
A fairy is a made-up creature. Fairies have wings and magical powers, and are often very small.

A fairy waves her wand to do magic things.

farm (noun)
A farm is a large piece of land with buildings on it. It is used for keeping animals and growing crops.

These farmers live on a farm, and look after their animals.

fall (verb)
To fall is to drop down quickly. If you fall, you might hurt yourself.

If you don't pick the apples, they will fall off the tree.

father (noun)
A father is a man who has one or more children.

Some children call their father "Dad" or "Daddy".

fear (verb)

To fear something is to be afraid of it because you think it might cause you pain or hurt.

The knight fears the dragon.

finger (noun)

A finger is part of your hand. You have four fingers and a thumb on each hand.

You can use your fingers to help you count.

feather (noun)

A feather is a soft object that grows out of a bird's skin. Feathers keep birds warm and dry.

This white feather came from a dove.

fire engine (noun)

A fire engine is a vehicle that goes to put out fires. Firefighters travel inside a fire engine.

This fire engine has a big ladder on the roof.

female (adjective)

A female person is a woman or a girl.

My sister and my aunt are both female.

fish (noun)

A fish is an animal that lives in water. Fish have fins and tails to help them swim.

A fish tank is called an aquarium.

fetch (verb)

To fetch is to go and get something, and then bring it back.

The dog ran off to fetch the ball.

flag (noun)

A flag is a piece of material with a pattern on it. Each country has its own flag.

Flags often hang on flagpoles and fly in the wind.

41

a b c d e **f** g h i j k l m n o p q r s t u v w x y z

a b c d e **f** g h i j k l m n o p q r s t u v w x y z

flower (noun)
A flower is the part of a plant that has petals and makes seeds. Most flowers are colourful and have a sweet smell.

I grow pink flowers in my garden.

forest (noun)
A forest is a place where lots of trees grow close together.

Forests can contain lots of different types of tree.

fly (noun)
A fly is a small insect with two wings.

The fly made a buzzing noise as it flew past me.

fork (noun)
A fork has sharp points on one end and a long handle. You use a fork to lift your food to your mouth when you eat.

My fork has a blue handle.

fly (verb)
To fly is to move through the air. Aeroplanes and most birds can fly.

A kite will fly on a windy day.

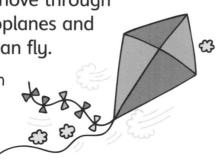

fossil (noun)
A fossil is part of a plant or an animal that lived a very long time ago, which has left its shape in a rock.

This fossil looks like a big snail.

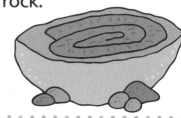

foal (noun)
A foal is a baby horse.

A foal stays with its mother. She keeps it safe.

fountain (noun)
A fountain is something that shoots water up into the air.

There is a big fountain at the park.

fox (noun)

A fox is a wild animal that looks like a dog with a thick, furry tail. Foxes usually sleep in the day.

A fox usually has red fur.

frown (verb)

A frown is the look on your face when you are angry, worried or thinking hard. When you frown your face gets lines on it.

My father frowns when he is cross with me.

friend (noun)

A friend is a person you like a lot. They are someone you know very well and who knows you well.

I sit next to my best friend at school.

fruit (noun)

A fruit is the part of a plant that has seeds in it and can be eaten as food. Most fruits are juicy and taste nice.

There is lots of fruit in this basket.

frog (noun)

A frog is a small animal with long back legs and slimy skin. Frogs usually live in or near water.

A green frog lives in our school pond.

full (adjective)

Something that is full has no space left inside it.

Your glass is full when the orange juice reaches the top.

frost (noun)

Frost is very thin ice that looks like powder. Frost is made when the weather is very cold.

The frost made patterns on the window.

funny (adjective)

A funny thing or person makes you laugh.

My comic book has funny stories in it.

Gg

gallop (verb)
When a horse gallops, it runs as fast as it can.

The horse had to gallop to win the race.

garden (noun)
A garden is the land around a house. People often have grass and plants in their garden.

We grow vegetables in our garden.

game (noun)
A game is an activity or sport that you play. A game has rules that tell you what you can do.

I played a game of tennis.

gate (noun)
A gate is a door in a fence, a hedge or a wall. A gate is usually made of wood or metal.

Our garden gate is blue.

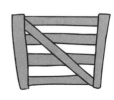

garage (noun)
A garage is a building where you park your car, or a place where you take your car to be mended.

My mum parks her car in the garage.

gentle (adjective)
Gentle means kind. Someone who is gentle is quiet and thoughtful.

This cat is gentle with her kittens.

44

gerbil (noun)

A gerbil is a very small, furry animal with a long tail.

Gerbils like to eat seeds and fruit.

giraffe (noun)

A giraffe is a tall animal with a very long neck. Giraffes live in Africa and they eat leaves.

The giraffe is yellow with brown patches.

ghost (noun)

Some people believe that a ghost is the spirit of a person who has died, returning to visit the living.

I dress up as a ghost for fancy-dress parties.

girl (noun)

A girl is a female child. When a girl grows up, she becomes a woman.

This is a baby girl. She is my sister.

giant (noun)

A giant is a very large and powerful person. Giants only exist in stories.

This giant is taller than a house.

give (verb)

To give means to hand something over to someone else.

I give my dad a card on his birthday.

gift (noun)

A gift is something that you give to, or receive from, someone.

I had lots of gifts to open on my birthday.

glass (noun)

Glass is a hard material that you can see through. Windows are made from glass.

Some glass is coloured, like this church window.

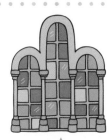

a b c d e f g h i j k l m n o p q r s t u v w x y z

glasses (noun)
Glasses are two pieces of glass or plastic inside a frame. You wear glasses over your eyes to help you see better.

The girl wears glasses when she reads.

gold (noun)
Gold is a shiny, yellow metal. It costs a lot of money.

Gold is used to make coins, rings, bracelets and earrings.

glove (noun)
A glove is a piece of clothing which covers your hand. It has a part for each finger and thumb.

I wear my green gloves when it is cold.

goodbye (noun)
You say goodbye when a person leaves. Sometimes you wave your hand when you say goodbye.

I wave goodbye to my dad at the train station.

glue (noun)
Glue is a thick liquid used to stick things together.

He used glue to stick the paper flowers on the sheet of paper.

goose (noun)
A goose is a large bird with a long neck. It is a good swimmer.

A goose honks and flaps its wings when it is angry.

goat (noun)
A goat is a farm animal. It is hairy and usually has horns on its head.

The goat is eating grass.

gorilla (noun)
A gorilla is a big, strong animal. Its fur is thick and dark.

Gorillas eat leaves and fruit.

grandfather (noun)

Your grandfather is the father of one of your parents. Some people call their grandfather "Grandad" or "Grandpa".

My grandfather is a good cook.

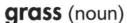

grass (noun)

Grass is a plant with very thin leaves which grow upwards. Grass often covers the ground in parks or gardens.

Most grass is green.

grandmother (noun)

Your grandmother is the mother of one of your parents. Some people call their grandmother "Granny" or "Grandma".

My grandmother reads me stories.

grow (verb)

To grow means to get bigger. Everything that is alive can grow.

The sunflowers in my garden grow taller every day.

grape (noun)

A grape is a small, sweet fruit. You can eat grapes, or use them to make juice.

Grapes grow in bunches on plants called vines.

guinea pig (noun)

A guinea pig is a small furry animal with no tail. You can keep guinea pigs as pets.

Guinea pigs like to eat lettuce.

grapefruit (noun)

A grapefruit is a round fruit with a thick skin. The inside of a grapefruit can be yellow, pink or red.

This grapefruit has been cut into two halves.

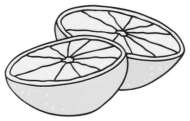

guitar (noun)

A guitar is a musical instrument. It has strings that you play with your fingers.

I have a brown guitar.

a b c d e f g h i j k l m n o p q r s t u v w x y z

Hh

hair (noun)

Hair is a soft, fine thread which grows out of skin. People and animals can have hair.

My hair is curly but my sister's hair is straight.

half (noun)

When you split something into two parts of the same size, each part is a half.

This pear has been cut in half.

hand (noun)

Your hand is the part of your body at the end of your arm. A hand has four fingers and a thumb.

My hand is a lot smaller than my mum's hand.

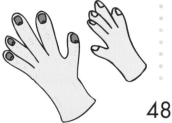

handle (noun)

A handle is the part of something you hold. You use a door handle to open and close the door.

My bag has two blue handles.

happy (adjective)

Feeling happy means being pleased about something. Happy is the opposite of sad.

The boy is happy because he won a medal.

hard (adjective)

Something hard is very solid and firm to touch. Hard is the opposite of soft.

A stone bench feels hard when you sit on it.

hare (noun)

A hare is a wild animal which looks like a big rabbit. A hare can run very fast.

I saw a hare out in the field.

hear (verb)

To hear means to listen to sounds. You hear with your ears.

The children could hear music from the radio.

hatch (verb)

To hatch means to come out of an egg.

The baby crocodile hatched from an egg.

heart (noun)

Your heart is an organ in your chest. It pumps blood around your body.

When you run fast, you can feel your heart beating.

hay (noun)

Hay is dry grass. You feed hay to animals such as horses and cows.

The hay is stored in the barn.

hedge (noun)

A hedge is a row of bushes that grow close together.

A bird has made a nest inside the hedge.

head (noun)

Your head is the part of your body containing your brain, eyes, ears, nose and mouth.

I wear a warm hat on my head when I go outside.

heel (noun)

Your heel is the back part of your foot below your ankle.

Your heel is at one end of your foot and your toes are at the other end.

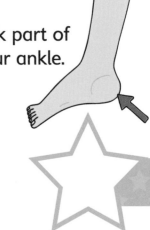

helicopter (noun)

A helicopter is a vehicle that flies. It has blades on the top that spin around.

A helicopter can fly straight up into the air.

high (adjective)

If something is high, it is a long way up from the ground.

A hot-air balloon flies high in the sky.

helmet (noun)

A helmet is a type of hard hat. You wear it to protect your head.

It's important to wear a helmet when you ride your bike.

hippopotamus (noun)

A hippopotamus is a large wild animal with short legs. Hippopotamuses are also called hippos.

The hippopotamus swims in the river.

help (verb)

To help is to do something useful for someone else.

I help my parents when they cook.

hit (verb)

To hit is to touch something quickly and firmly.

I hit the tennis ball with my tennis racket.

hide (verb)

To hide means to put something in a place where no one can see it.

My sister hides her diary in a box.

hold (verb)

When you hold something you keep it in your hand or arms.

I hold my big brother's hand when I cross the road.

holiday (noun)

A holiday is a special day or trip. You don't usually work or go to school on a holiday.

Today is a holiday, so we are going to the beach!

house (noun)

A house is a place where people live. It is usually made of stone, bricks or wood.

My house has a blue front door.

hollow (adjective)

If something is hollow it is empty inside.

This tube is hollow.

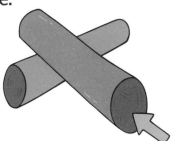

hug (verb)

To hug is to put your arms around someone or something to show that you like them.

I hug my baby brother before I go to bed.

honey (noun)

Honey is a sweet food made by bees.

My sister puts honey on her toast.

hungry (adjective)

Being hungry is the feeling of wanting to eat food.

Do you feel hungry at lunchtime?

horse (noun)

A horse is a large animal with a tail and a mane. Horses can move quickly and are often ridden by people.

I put a saddle on the horse.

hurry (verb)

To hurry means to move, or go somewhere, quickly.

We had to hurry to catch the train!

Ii

ice cream (noun)

Ice cream is a cold, sweet food. It is made from frozen cream and sugar.

My brother likes strawberry ice cream.

Internet (noun)

The Internet is a system that links computers all over the world.

The Internet makes it easy to talk to my grandparents.

insect (noun)

An insect is a tiny animal with six legs.

Wasps, ants and ladybirds are insects.

invite (verb)

To invite means to ask someone to do something or go somewhere.

I'm going to invite my friends to a party.

instrument (noun)

An instrument is something you play to make music.

The trumpet and the guitar are instruments.

island (noun)

An island is a piece of land with water on all sides of it.

You can travel all the way around the island in a boat.

Jj

jacket (noun)

A jacket is a piece of clothing that goes over a top or dress. A jacket usually has sleeves and opens at the front.

I have a blue jacket.

join (verb)

To join means to put two things together.

I can join these puzzle pieces together.

jeans (noun)

Jeans are trousers. They are made from a blue cloth called denim.

Both my brother and my sister like to wear jeans.

juice (noun)

Juice is the liquid that can be squeezed from solid foods such as fruits or vegetables.

We drink orange juice with breakfast.

jellyfish (noun)

A jellyfish is an animal that lives in the sea. It has a soft body.

A jellyfish has lots of long arms, called tentacles.

jump (verb)

To jump means to push your body into the air, so that your feet are off the ground.

Do you like to jump on a trampoline?

Kk

kangaroo (noun)
A kangaroo is an animal that lives in Australia. It has strong back legs so it can jump a long way.

The kangaroo lives in the outback.

keyboard (noun)
A keyboard is a panel of buttons. Computers, phones and pianos all have a keyboard.

I use my computer keyboard to type messages.

kennel (noun)
A kennel is a place for a dog to stay. A kennel often looks like a small house.

Our dog sleeps in a kennel at night.

kick (verb)
When you kick something, you hit it hard with your foot.

My brother can kick a ball a long way!

key (noun)
A key is a small object which is used to open a lock or start a car.

Most keys are made of metal.

kind (adjective)
Being kind means thinking of other people and trying to help them.

It is kind to give flowers to someone who is ill.

king (noun)

A king is a man who is part of a royal family and who rules a country.

The king wears a crown.

kitten (noun)

A kitten is a young cat. A mother cat looks after her kittens.

Our cat has four kittens.

kiss (verb)

To kiss means to touch someone or something with your lips.

I kiss my grandma when she comes to visit.

knee (noun)

Your knee is the part of your body in the middle of your leg. Your knee is where your leg bends.

This dancer is bending her knee.

kitchen (noun)

A kitchen is the room food is cooked in.

I like to cook with my dad in the kitchen.

knife (noun)

A knife has a handle and a blade that is usually sharp on one side. You use a knife to cut something.

I use a knife and fork to eat my lunch.

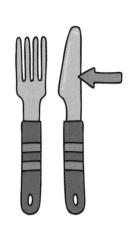

kite (noun)

A kite is a toy made from fabric or paper stretched over a frame, tied to a long piece of string.

We fly kites at the park on windy days.

koala (noun)

A koala is a grey, furry animal that lives in Australia. It has a black nose and round ears.

Koalas live in trees and eat leaves.

a b c d e f g h i j k l m n o p q r s t u v w x y z

Ll

label (noun)

A label is a small piece of paper or card attached to something. It shows useful information.

These labels show what is in each jar.

lake (noun)

A lake is an area of water with land around it.

The lake is in a forest.

ladder (noun)

A ladder is a set of steps held between two poles. You use a ladder to reach high places.

The ladder is made of wood.

lamb (noun)

A lamb is a baby sheep. Lambs live on farms.

The lamb likes to skip and play.

ladybird (noun)

A ladybird is an insect that can fly. A ladybird is usually brightly coloured with spots.

The ladybird is red with black spots.

lamp (noun)

A lamp is a thing that gives off light. You can switch a lamp on and off.

I have a lamp next to my bed.

56

large (adjective)
If something is large it means that it is big. Large is the opposite of small.

An elephant is a large animal.

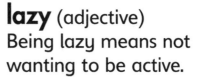

lazy (adjective)
Being lazy means not wanting to be active.

When I feel lazy, I don't want to get up and play outside.

late (adjective)
You are late when you arrive somewhere after the time you are expected.

You may have to run so you are not late.

leaf (noun)
A leaf is the flat part of a plant or tree which grows from a branch or stem.

When the summer ends, this green leaf will turn red.

laugh (verb)
To laugh means to smile and make a sound that shows you are happy.

Clowns make us laugh!

learn (verb)
To learn means to find out something that you did not know before.

Children need to learn how to spell.

lawn (noun)
A lawn is an area of cut grass. Gardens and parks often have lawns.

My mum uses a lawnmower to cut the grass on the lawn.

leave (verb)
To leave means to go away from somewhere or someone.

She is leaving to go on holiday.

a b c d e f g h i j k l m n o p q r s t u v w x y z

Left is the opposite side to right. You have a left hand and a right hand.

Katie holds up her left hand.

lift (verb)

When you lift something, you pick it up with your hands.

I'm helping my brother lift a box.

leg (noun)

Your leg is the part of your body that allows you to stand, walk, run and climb.

You have two legs, but many animals have four legs.

light (adjective)

Light means little or no darkness. When it is light, you can see what is around you.

It was light outside when I woke up.

lemon (noun)

A lemon is a sour yellow fruit. Lemons grow on trees in hot countries.

We use lemons to make a drink called lemonade.

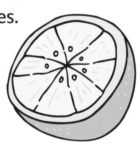

light (noun)

A light is an object that helps you to see in the dark. Most lights have electric bulbs in them.

The car has lights at the front and the back.

leopard (noun)

A leopard is a type of large, wild cat. It has dark spots and sharp teeth and claws.

The leopard is sitting in a tree.

lion (noun)

A lion is a type of large, wild cat that lives in Africa. Male lions have manes around their face.

A baby lion is called a cub.

liquid (noun)

A liquid is something which flows freely. A liquid cannot be solid.

Water and milk are both liquids.

lose (verb)

If you lose something, you cannot find it.

My uncle has lost his keys.

little (adjective)

If something is little it is small in size.

My sister has a little puppy.

loud (adjective)

Loud means to make a lot of noise. If you hit a drum you make a loud sound.

I put my hands over my ears when my sister makes a loud noise.

long (adjective)

If something is long it is not short.

The monkey wraps its long tail around a branch.

love (verb)

To love someone or something means to like that person or thing a lot.

I love my cat.

look (verb)

To look means to use your eyes to see something.

My aunt is looking at her cat.

low (adjective)

Low means near the ground. Low is the opposite of high.

There is a low wall around the fountain.

a b c d e f g h i j k **l** m n o p q r s t u v w x y z

Mm

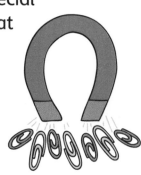

machine (noun)
A machine is an object made to do a specific job. Machines have more than one part.

A hairdryer is a machine that blows hot air.

magnet (noun)
A magnet is a special piece of metal that pulls other metal things towards it.

A magnet can pick up paper clips.

magazine (noun)
A magazine is a very thin book with pictures and stories in it. It is usually sold weekly or monthly.

My grandmother reads a magazine about houses.

make (verb)
To make something means to build or create it by putting other things together.

Can you make a tower with bricks?

magic (noun)
Magic is the power that makes something impossible happen.

The fairy used her wand to make magic.

male (adjective)
A male person is a man or a boy.

My brothers and my uncle are both male.

mammal (noun)

A mammal is an animal that feeds its babies milk and usually has hair or fur.

Deer, cats, donkeys and people are all mammals.

mask (noun)

A mask is an object you wear over your face. It can protect or hide your face.

The pink mask goes over your eyes.

man (noun)

A man is a grown-up male person. When a boy grows up he becomes a man.

My father is a man.

mast (noun)

A mast is a tall pole that holds up the sails on a boat.

Long ago, some sailing boats had three tall masts.

mane (noun)

A mane is the long hair that grows on the neck of some mammals.

I comb my horse's mane to make him look smart.

meal (noun)

A meal is the food you eat at a certain time of day. A meal contains more than one type of food.

My favourite meal is breakfast.

map (noun)

A map is a drawing that shows you where places are. You can use a map to plan a journey.

I can follow the river on the map.

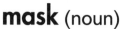

mean (adjective)

To be mean is to be nasty to someone. If someone is mean, they are not being kind.

Laughing at somebody who is hurt is mean.

a b c d e f g h i j k l m n o p q r s t u v w x y z

measure (verb)
To measure is to find out how big or how heavy something is.

I measure my little brother with a height chart.

melon (noun)
A melon is a large, sweet fruit. It is round and usually has a yellow or green skin.

My mum cuts a melon into slices to eat it.

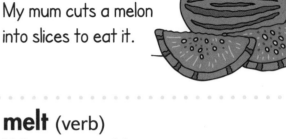

medal (noun)
A medal is a small, shiny metal object given to celebrate something, such as winning a race.

My sister won a medal at sports day.

melt (verb)
When something melts it changes to a liquid. Heat makes things melt.

Ice cream melts if you don't eat it quickly!

medicine (noun)
Medicine is the item you are given when you feel ill, to help you get better.

The doctor gave me some medicine when I had a sore throat.

mermaid (noun)
A mermaid is a made-up sea creature which looks like a woman who has a tail like a fish.

In stories, mermaids often have long, curly hair.

medium (adjective)
Medium is the size between big and small.

I am not very tall or very short, so I am a medium height.

message (noun)
A message is information, usually words, that you send to someone.

I send messages to my friends by email.

milk (noun)

Milk is a white liquid that comes from some female animals. Cows and goats both make milk.

My sister and I drink milk before bed.

mix (verb)

To mix means to put two or more things together to make something else.

You can mix blue and red paints to make purple.

mirror (noun)

A mirror is a special piece of glass that reflects images. You can see yourself in a mirror.

My mum looks in the mirror when she brushes her hair.

moat (noun)

A moat is a deep, narrow ditch which goes around a castle. A moat is usually filled with water.

The moat protected the castle from attacks.

miss (verb)

If you miss something then you do not catch, hit or get it.

The tennis player missed the ball.

money (noun)

Money is used to buy things. Money is usually made of metal coins or pieces of paper called notes.

I save my money in a piggy bank.

mistake (noun)

A mistake is something that is wrong. It is something that you did not mean to do.

The teacher marked my mistake with a big red X.

monkey (noun)

A monkey is a wild, hairy animal with long arms, legs and a tail.

This monkey lives in the jungle.

monster (noun)
A monster is a scary, made-up creature which only exists in stories.

This monster has big horns on its head.

moth (noun)
A moth is a flying insect that looks like a butterfly. Moths are often less colourful than butterflies.

Moths are attracted to light.

month (noun)
A month is a period of time. Every year has 12 months in it. Each month has a name.

The calendar shows what month it is.

May

	1	2	3	4	5
6	7	8	9	10	11	12
13	14	15	16	17	18	19
20	21	22	23	24	25	26
27	28	29	30	31		

mother (noun)
A mother is a woman who has one or more children. Another word for mother is mum.

My mother likes to play the piano.

moon (noun)
A moon is a large round object that circles a planet. The Earth has one moon.

I can see the Moon at night from my bedroom window.

motorbike (noun)
A motorbike is a vehicle with two wheels and an engine.

My aunt rides a motorbike to work.

morning (noun)
The morning is the first half of each day. The morning ends at 12 o'clock, in the middle of the day.

We eat our breakfast in the morning.

mountain (noun)
A mountain is a very high hill. There is sometimes snow at the top of mountains.

Explorers climb mountains all over the world.

mouse (noun)

A mouse is a small, furry animal with a long tail.

This mouse has a long, pink tail.

mug (noun)

A mug is a big cup with a handle. Mugs are usually used for hot drinks.

My mug has stripes on it but my friend's mug has spots.

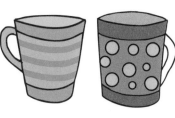

mouth (noun)

Your mouth is the part of your face that you use for talking and eating.

I open my mouth wide when I sing!

multiply (verb)

To multiply means to make something bigger by adding more of it.

If you multiply 5 by 2, the answer is 10.

move (verb)

To move means to make something go from one place to another.

We are moving when we walk.

muscle (noun)

A muscle is a part of your body inside your skin. You use your muscles to help you move.

Acrobats have very strong muscles.

mud (noun)

Mud is wet soil.

When it rains, we get mud on our boots.

music (noun)

Music is the sound you make when you sing or play an instrument.

The girl played beautiful music on her violin.

65

Nn

name (noun)

A name is the word you use to talk about someone or something. Your name is what people call you.

My name is Anna and my kitten's name is Paws.

needle (noun)

A needle is a very thin piece of metal used for sewing, with a sharp point at one end and a very small hole at the other end.

This needle has blue thread in it.

naughty (adjective)

If someone is naughty they do not behave well. Naughty means doing things you are told not to do.

The naughty puppy chewed my teddy.

neighbour (noun)

A neighbour is a person who lives next door to you, or very near you.

I talk to my neighbour over the fence.

neck (noun)

Your neck is the part of your body between your head and your shoulders.

My mum wears a sparkly necklace around her neck.

nest (noun)

A nest is a home that birds and mice build. They usually build nests with twigs, grass and leaves.

Birds build their nests in trees.

net (noun)
A net is an object used to catch fish. It usually has a long handle and a soft basket made from string.

We take a net when we go to the beach!

nose (noun)
Your nose is the part of your face that you breathe and smell through.

My brother has freckles on his nose.

new (adjective)
If something is new it has only just been made or used. New is the opposite of old.

My new trainers are cleaner than my old trainers.

note (noun)
A note is a short message that you write to someone, often as a letter.

I wrote a note to say thank you for my present.

night (noun)
Night is the time between the evening and the morning. At night it is usually dark outside.

I can see the stars at night.

nurse (noun)
A nurse looks after people who are ill. Most nurses work in hospitals.

The nurse put a bandage on my arm.

noise (noun)
A noise is a sound you hear. If a noise is loud, it might make you jump.

An aeroplane makes a loud noise.

nut (noun)
A nut is a fruit with a hard shell. You need to take off the shell before you eat most nuts.

My favourite nuts are hazelnuts, but my dad likes walnuts.

a b c d e f g h i j k l m n o p q r s t u v w x y z

Oo

oar (noun)
An oar is a wooden pole with one flat end. Oars are used to make small boats move on water.

We need two oars to row this boat.

ocean (noun)
An ocean is a large area of water which is part of the sea.

The Pacific Ocean is the largest ocean in the world.

oats (noun)
Oats are the seeds of a cereal plant. Farmers grow oats in fields.

We use oats to make porridge.

octopus (noun)
An octopus is an animal that lives in the ocean. It has a soft body and eight arms.

The octopus uses its arms to swim.

obey (verb)
If you obey someone, you do what that person tells you to do.

The sheepdog obeyed the farmer and sat down.

office (noun)
An office is a place where people go to work. In an office you often sit at a desk.

My mum works in an office.

oil (noun)
Oil is a thick liquid. Some oils are used to make machines work; others are used for cooking.

We have olive oil in our kitchen.

opposite (noun)
Opposite is something that is very different from another thing. Hot is the opposite of cold.

Wet is the opposite of dry.

old (adjective)
If something is old it was made a long time ago, or has been used many times. Old is the opposite of new.

My old jumper has a hole in it.

orange (noun)
An orange is a round, juicy fruit. You peel off the thick skin, and eat the soft parts inside.

We all eat oranges after football matches.

omelette (noun)
An omelette is a food made from eggs which are beaten and fried in a pan.

I like cheese and tomatoes in my omelette.

orchard (noun)
An orchard is a place where fruit trees grow.

There are pear trees in the orchard.

open (adjective)
Open means not shut. If something is open, it is not shut or closed.

If the front door is open, you can walk into the house.

owl (noun)
An owl is a bird with large, round eyes. It hunts at night and catches mice, frogs and insects to eat.

The owl waited in the tree.

Pp

padlock (noun)

A padlock is a small metal lock. You can use it to lock gates and cupboards.

You need a key to open this padlock.

paint (verb)

To paint is the action of putting paint on a piece of paper or on walls.

We used big brushes to paint the walls of my room.

page (noun)

A page is a piece of paper. A page is often part of a book or magazine.

There are pictures and words on this page.

pair (noun)

A pair is two things that are the same, or that go together.

My friend is wearing a pair of red shoes.

paint (noun)

Paint is a coloured liquid which dries on a surface, such as paper. You use paints and a brush to make a picture.

I used blue and yellow paint to make a picture.

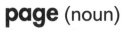

pancake (noun)

A pancake is a thin, flat food. It is made from eggs, flour and milk mixed together and fried.

My sister likes blueberries with her pancakes.

panda (noun)

A panda is a wild, black and white bear which lives in China.

This panda family is eating bamboo.

park (noun)

A park is a large area where people walk and play. It has grass, trees and flowers but no houses.

We go to the park to play on the swings.

paper (noun)

Paper is a thin sheet of material made from trees. You can write, draw or paint on paper.

I used paper to write a letter to my friend.

park (verb)

To park means to leave a vehicle somewhere. A special area made only for parking is called a car park.

We usually park our car outside our house.

parachute (noun)

A parachute is an object that helps people fall slowly and safely when they jump out of a plane.

The parachute is attached with strong ropes.

parrot (noun)

A parrot is a bird with colourful feathers and a hooked beak. Parrots live in warm countries.

The parrot has a blue tail and red wings.

parent (noun)

A parent is a person who has a child. A parent can be a man or a woman.

My parents wave goodbye when I go to school.

party (noun)

A party is a time when a group of people have fun together.

Your friends come to a party on your birthday.

passenger (noun)
A passenger is someone who travels in a vehicle but is not the driver.

When I get the train I am a passenger.

pea (noun)
A pea is a green vegetable. Peas are small and round.

Peas grow inside a little case called a pod.

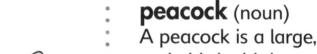

passport (noun)
A passport is a special little book with your picture in it. You usually need one to visit another country.

I used my passport when we went on holiday.

peacock (noun)
A peacock is a large, male bird with beautiful feathers. A female peacock is called a peahen.

The peacock spreads out the feathers in his tail.

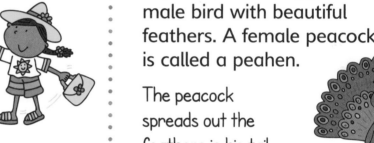

pasta (noun)
Pasta is a food made from flour and water. It comes in lots of shapes and is usually boiled before eating.

My dad cooks pasta with tomato sauce and cheese.

peanut (noun)
A peanut is a seed that you can eat. A peanut is also known as a groundnut.

I sometimes have to break peanuts out of their shells to eat them.

paw (noun)
A paw is the foot of an animal. Some animals' paws have sharp claws.

The cat licked her paw.

pear (noun)
A pear is a juicy fruit that grows on a tree. It has a green or yellow skin.

I ate a pear after lunch.

pebble (noun)

A pebble is a small, round stone. You can find pebbles near areas of water like rivers.

These pebbles do not have any sharp edges.

pencil (noun)

A pencil is an object like a thin stick with a grey or coloured centre. They are used to write or draw.

I sharpened my pencil so I could draw a thin line.

pedal (noun)

A pedal is a flat object that you push with your feet to make a machine do something.

There are two pedals on my bike.

penguin (noun)

A penguin is a black and white bird. Penguins cannot fly, but they can dive and swim.

Most penguins live in very cold places near the sea.

peel (verb)

To peel means to take the skin off a fruit or vegetable.

You need to peel bananas and oranges to eat them.

perform (verb)

To perform means to act, sing or dance in front of other people.

We performed our school play for lots of people.

pen (noun)

A pen is an object with ink inside it. Pens are used to write or draw.

My sister uses a pen to write in her diary.

perfume (noun)

Perfume is a liquid which smells nice. Perfume can be sprayed on skin or clothes so they smell good.

My mum wears perfume on special days.

person (noun)
A person is a man, woman or child.

When I see a person I know, I wave hello.

picnic (noun)
A picnic is a meal that you eat outside, often away from home.

We took our picnic to the beach.

pet (noun)
A pet is an animal that you keep at home. You care for your pet, and keep it safe and well.

My dog and my cat are both pets.

picture (noun)
A picture is a drawing, a painting or a photograph.

We have lots of pictures hanging on the wall.

photograph (noun)
A photograph is a picture that you take with a camera. A photograph is also called a photo.

This is a photograph of my twin sisters.

pie (noun)
A pie is a type of food with pastry on the outside and meat or fruit in the middle.

I ate a slice of apple pie.

piano (noun)
A piano is a large musical instrument. It has a keyboard of black and white keys.

My brother plays the piano.

pig (noun)
A pig is a farm animal with a curly tail and short legs. A baby pig is called a piglet.

Most pigs are pink.

pigeon (noun)

A pigeon is a grey bird. It has a small head and a round body.

The pigeons peck at food on the ground.

pipe (noun)

A pipe is a long, hollow tube made of plastic or metal. Things, such as liquids, can move through pipes.

A pipe carries water to the tap.

pillow (noun)

A pillow is a bag filled with soft material that you rest your head on when you go to sleep.

Our cat sleeps on my pillow with me.

pirate (noun)

A pirate is a person who attacks a ship and steals things from it.

The pirate wore a big blue hat.

pilot (noun)

A pilot is a person who flies an aeroplane.

Pilots wear a smart uniform.

pizza (noun)

Pizza is a food made of a bread crust topped with tomato and cheese. Other food can be added as toppings.

I like ham and pineapple pizza.

pineapple (noun)

A pineapple is a yellow fruit. The skin is hard and prickly, but the inside is juicy and sweet.

I love to eat pineapple with my friends.

plain (adjective)

If something is plain it has no decoration on it.

I wear plain black socks to school.

planet (noun)
A planet is a giant, round object that moves around a star. We live on the planet Earth.

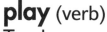

Earth moves around a star called the Sun.

play (verb)
To play means to do something fun with your friends, or with your toys.

My little sister likes to play with building blocks.

plant (noun)
A plant is a living thing that is not an animal. Trees, bushes and garden flowers are plants.

Most plants are green.

playground (noun)
A playground is a special area outside where children can play.

Our school playground has a slide and swings.

plant (verb)
To plant means to put seeds or plants into the ground to grow.

I planted some sunflower seeds. Look what grew!

plum (noun)
A plum is a soft fruit with a stone in the middle. Plums can be red, green, yellow or purple.

We picked a basket of juicy plums.

plastic (noun)
Plastic is a strong material that is used to make many different things.

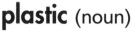

Spoons, bottles and buckets can be made of plastic.

pocket (noun)
A pocket is a small bag that is sewn into your clothes. You put things in a pocket.

I have some coins and pencils in my pockets.

polar bear (noun)

A polar bear is a large, white bear. Polar bears live in very cold places.

Polar bears are the biggest bears in the world.

poppy (noun)

A poppy is a plant that grows large flowers. Most poppy flowers are red.

Wild poppies can grow in fields.

pond (noun)

A pond is a small area of still water with land all around it. A pond is much smaller than a lake.

We have frogs in our school pond.

porcupine (noun)

A porcupine is an animal with long, sharp hairs on its back. The hairs are called quills.

The porcupine uses its quills to scare other animals.

pony (noun)

A pony is a small type of horse.

I learned to ride on a pony.

portrait (noun)

A portrait is a picture of someone. A portrait can be a drawing, a painting or a photograph.

There was a portrait of the queen on the wall.

popcorn (noun)

Popcorn is a snack food made from pieces of corn that pop open when they are heated.

I eat popcorn when I go to the cinema.

postcard (noun)

A postcard is a small piece of card that you write a message on and post to someone.

I sent a postcard from New York.

a b c d e f g h i j k l m n o p q r s t u v w x y z

potato (noun)
A potato is a vegetable that grows under the ground. It usually has red or brown skin, and is white on the inside.

You can make chips and crisps from potatoes.

prize (noun)
A prize is something that you give to a person who wins a race or a competition.

The first prize was a medal.

practise (verb)
To practise means to do something lots of times to help you get better at it.

I practise the violin every day.

promise (verb)
To promise means to say that you will definitely do something.

I promised to help with the washing-up each day.

prince (noun)
A prince is the son of a king or a queen.

The prince likes to ride his horse.

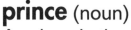

puddle (noun)
A puddle is a little pool of liquid. Rain makes lots of puddles of water.

My puppy loves to splash in puddles.

princess (noun)
A princess is the daughter of a king or a queen.

The princess likes to write stories.

pull (verb)
To pull means to take hold of something and move it towards you.

I pulled the door open.

78

pump (noun)

A pump is a machine that pushes air or liquid in or out.

We used a pump to put air into my bicycle tyres.

push (verb)

To push is to take hold of something and move it away from you.

She pushes the toy train along the track.

pumpkin (noun)

A pumpkin is a large fruit with an orange skin. You can use pumpkins to make pie or soup.

You can carve a face into a hollowed-out pumpkin.

put (verb)

To put means to place something somewhere.

The librarian put the books on the desk.

puppet (noun)

A puppet is a toy person or animal that you can move using strings or your hand.

I can make this puppet walk, run and dance.

pyramid (noun)

A pyramid is a building whose sides join at the top in a point. The base is square and the other sides are triangles.

The pyramids in Egypt were built long ago.

puppy (noun)

A puppy is a young dog.

The puppy likes to play with other puppies.

python (noun)

A python is a large snake. It wraps its long body around branches.

This jungle python can slither and swim.

a b c d e f g h i j k l m n o p q r s t u v w x y z

Qq

quack (verb)
A quack is the noise a duck makes.

The mother duck quacks, and her ducklings follow her.

quarter (noun)
When you cut something into four equal parts, each part is a quarter.

The cake is cut into quarters.

qualify (verb)
To qualify means to win a competition or pass a test in order to get to the next stage.

Because I won the semi-final race I qualify for the final.

quarter (noun)
A quarter is a coin in North America. It is worth 25 cents, or one quarter of a dollar.

A US quarter has a picture of an eagle on one side.

quality (noun)
Quality is the word used to describe how good, or how bad, something is.

The red toy car is good quality because it has not broken.

queen (noun)
A queen is a woman who is part of a royal family and is the head of a country.

The queen wears a crown.

80

question (noun)

You ask a question when you want to find out about something. "What time is it?" is a question.

When you write a question down, you put a question mark at the end.

quilt (noun)

A quilt is a soft, warm covering for a bed. Some quilts are made of lots of squares of material sewn together, called patchwork.

My quilt keeps me cosy at night.

queue (noun)

A queue is a line of people who are waiting for something. It is pronounced like the letter 'q'.

There was a queue at the bus stop.

quit (verb)

To quit means to stop doing something.

She quit acrobatics when she broke her arm.

quick (adjective)

If something is quick, it is very fast. Quick is the opposite of slow.

He was quick to finish the race.

quiz (noun)

A quiz is a game where people answer questions. The person who gets the most answers correct is the winner.

I like to watch quiz shows on the television.

quiet (adjective)

If you are quiet you make no noise, or only a little noise. Quiet means not loud.

Shhh! You must be quiet when the baby is sleeping.

quote (verb)

To quote means to repeat something word for word.

The teacher quoted from the book.

a b c d e f g h i j k l m n o p q r s t u v w x y z

Rr

rabbit (noun)
A rabbit is a furry animal with long ears and a short, fluffy tail.

Rabbits eat grass and vegetables.

race (noun)
A race is an event held to find out who is the fastest at something. There are lots of different types of races.

The first to finish a race is the winner.

racing car (noun)
A racing car is a very fast car used in driving races.

The racing cars went around the track.

radiator (noun)
A radiator is an object that lets out heat to make a place warm. Most radiators are fitted to walls.

My room is warm because the radiator is on.

radio (noun)
A radio is a small machine made of metal or plastic which is used to listen to music or talk shows.

I listen to music on the radio.

rain (noun)
Rain is water that falls from the sky as small drops. Rain comes from clouds.

The rain fell for an hour.

rainbow (noun)

Rainbows are curved bands of colour that appear in the sky when the sun shines through raindrops.

We saw a rainbow in the sky.

reach (verb)

To reach is to stretch out your arm to get something.

I have to reach up high to get something from a top shelf.

raspberry (noun)

A raspberry is a small, red fruit. Raspberries grow on bushes.

I like to eat juicy raspberries.

read (verb)

To read means to look at words and know what they mean.

I sit in an armchair when I read a story.

rat (noun)

A rat is an animal that looks like a large mouse. Most rats are brown or black.

Rats have whiskers and long tails.

receipt (noun)

A receipt is a piece of paper that tells you how much money you have paid for something.

She gave me a receipt when I bought new books.

rattle (noun)

A rattle is a small toy for a baby. Rattles make a noise when you shake them.

My baby brother plays with a rattle.

recipe (noun)

A recipe is a set of instructions that tells you how to cook something.

I followed a recipe to make chocolate-chip cookies.

recorder (noun)

A recorder is a musical instrument with small holes along the body and a mouthpiece at the top. You blow into the mouthpiece to make a sound.

I play the recorder at school.

reindeer (noun)

A reindeer is a deer with large antlers on its head. Reindeer usually live in cold countries.

These reindeer are playing in the snow.

recycle (verb)

When you recycle something, you use it again or make something new from it.

We wash bottles before we recycle them.

remember (verb)

To remember means to think of something and not forget it.

I remember to brush my teeth every day.

reflection (noun)

A reflection is what you see when you look in a mirror or shiny surface.

The cat was surprised by its own reflection.

remove (verb)

To remove something means to take it away.

The men removed the heavy mirror from the wall.

refrigerator (noun)

A refrigerator is a machine that keeps food cold. It is also called a fridge.

Food stays cool and fresh inside a refrigerator.

repair (verb)

To repair means to fix something that is broken, so that it works again.

We use special tools to repair my bike.

reptile (noun)

A reptile is an animal with a scaly skin. Most reptiles lay eggs.

Snakes, lizards, crocodiles and tortoises are reptiles.

rhinoceros (noun)

A rhinoceros is a large, wild animal with one or two horns on the front of its head.

A rhinoceros is also called a rhino.

rescue (verb)

To rescue means to save someone (or something) from danger.

The firefighter rescued the kitten from the tree.

ribbon (noun)

A ribbon is a long, thin piece of material. You use a ribbon to tie something or to make it look nice.

The flowers are tied with a red ribbon.

restaurant (noun)

A restaurant is a place where you go to buy and eat a meal.

We went to a pizza restaurant for my birthday.

rice (noun)

Rice is a plant that produces tiny seeds, which are also called rice. You can cook and eat rice.

I can eat rice with two chopsticks!

reward (noun)

A reward is something given to a person for doing good work.

My teacher gave me a reward because I got all the answers right.

ride (verb)

To ride means to sit on, or in, something as it moves along. You ride on a horse by sitting on its back.

I went for a ride in the car.

a b c d e f g h i j k l m n o p q **r** s t u v w x y z

right (adjective)
Right can mean correct. Right is the opposite of wrong.

A tick shows that the answer is right.

roar (verb)
A roar is a deep, rumbling sound, usually made by an animal.

I heard the lion roar as loud as he could.

right (adjective)
Right is also the opposite side to left. You have a right hand and a left hand.

Do you hold a pencil with your right hand, or your left hand?

robot (noun)
A robot is a machine that does jobs for us. Robots are often controlled by computers.

This robot is painting a new car.

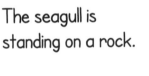

river (noun)
A river is a large stream of water that flows over land. Most rivers flow into the sea.

Fish live in this river.

rock (noun)
A rock is a very large, heavy stone.

The seagull is standing on a rock.

road (noun)
A road is a long stretch of ground that vehicles drive along. The surface of a road is hard.

The mother and son wait to cross the road.

rocket (noun)
A rocket is an object or machine that can fly upwards into space from the ground. Some types of rocket take people into space.

A rocket makes a lot of noise!

rocking chair (noun)

A rocking chair is a type of chair which has curved pieces of wood below its legs, to make it move backwards and forwards.

I like to sit in a rocking chair to read.

roof (noun)

A roof is the object that covers the top of a building. The roof sits on top of the walls.

Birds like to sit on the roof of this house.

rocking horse (noun)

A rocking horse is a wooden toy horse which moves backwards and forwards when you sit on it.

It's fun to ride on a rocking horse.

room (noun)

A room is a space inside a building. It has walls, a door and a floor.

A doll's house has rooms and windows, just like a real house.

roll (verb)

To roll means to turn over and over.

A ball will roll along the ground if you push it.

rope (noun)

Rope is very thick, strong string.

Lots of threads are twisted together to make a rope.

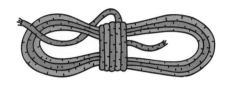

roller skate (noun)

A roller skate is a boot with a row of wheels on the bottom.

We wear kneepads with our roller skates, in case we fall over.

rose (noun)

A rose is a flower. It grows on a bush with thorns. Most roses smell nice.

This rose has red petals.

rough (adjective)

If something is rough it is bumpy and not smooth.

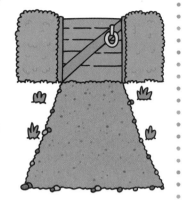

The path was rough and full of stones.

rug (noun)

A rug is a thick mat. Rugs are usually used to cover areas of floor.

The rug in my bedroom is pink to match the walls.

round (adjective)

If something is round, it is shaped like a circle or a ball. Something round has no corners.

There are two round balloons at the party.

ruler (noun)

A ruler is a flat piece of wood or plastic with marks along the side, used to draw straight lines and to measure things.

I used my ruler to draw a square.

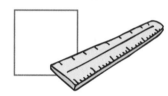

row (noun)

A row is a straight line of people or things.

The teacher put the chairs in a row.

run (verb)

To run means to move very quickly on your legs. Running is faster than walking.

A cheetah can run faster than any other animal.

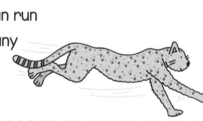

row (verb)

To row a boat means to move it along by pulling and pushing oars.

He had to row across the lake.

runway (noun)

A runway is a long, wide area at an airport. It is where aeroplanes take off and land.

The plane landed on the runway.

88

Ss

saddle (noun)
A saddle is the seat you sit on when you ride a horse or a bicycle.

My bike has a comfy saddle.

sandal (noun)
A sandal is a light shoe held on with straps. Sandals keep your feet cool in warm weather.

When I wear my sandals I can see my toes.

sail (noun)
A sail is a piece of material that is fixed to a boat. Wind fills the sail and makes the boat move.

This boat has two sails.

sandcastle (noun)
A sandcastle is a small castle made of wet sand. You use a bucket and spade to build a sandcastle.

The sea washed the sandcastle away.

salad (noun)
A salad is a dish of uncooked vegetables, such as lettuce, tomato and cucumber.

Would you like a salad for dinner?

sandwich (noun)
A sandwich is two pieces of bread with food held between them.

I had a cheese and tomato sandwich for my lunch.

89

a b c d e f g h i j k l m n o p q r **s** t u v w x y z

scales (noun)
You use scales to find out how heavy something is.

I put cherries on the scales to weigh them.

school (noun)
A school is a place where children go to learn to read and write.

I have lots of friends at school.

scare (verb)
To scare someone, or something, means to make them feel frightened.

Spiders and snakes really scare me!

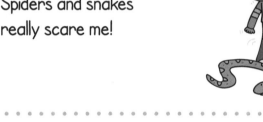

scissors (noun)
Scissors are used for cutting things. They have two blades that open and close when you move the ring-shaped handles.

The girl cut out paper shapes with her scissors.

scarecrow (noun)
A scarecrow is a model man made from sticks and straw. It is put in a field to scare birds away from crops.

The farmer dresses his scarecrow in old clothes.

screwdriver (noun)
A screwdriver is a tool for fitting a screw. It has a handle and a metal rod with a shaped end that fits into a screw.

You turn a screwdriver to tighten or loosen a screw.

scarf (noun)
A scarf is a long, woolly strip that you wear around your neck to keep you warm.

I wear my hat and scarf when it snows.

sea (noun)
The sea is the big area of salty water that surrounds the land.

Ships and boats sail across the sea.

seahorse (noun)

A seahorse is a small fish with a curly tail and a head shaped like a horse's head.

Seahorses swim upright, fluttering their fins to move along.

seaweed (noun)

Seaweed is a plant that grows in the sea.

The seaweed on the rocks is very slippery.

seal (noun)

A seal is a wild animal that lives in the sea and on the seashore. It has flippers to help it swim.

Seals catch fish to eat.

seed (noun)

A seed is an object made by a plant. It can grow into a new plant.

I am planting my lettuce seeds in the garden.

seat (noun)

A seat is something you sit on, such as a chair or a stool.

There are three empty seats around the table.

see-saw (noun)

A see-saw is a long board that you can play on. A child sits at each end and pushes off the ground with their feet to move up and down.

Is there a see-saw in a park near you?

seat belt (noun)

A seat belt is a strap that you wear in a vehicle. It fastens across your body to help keep you safe.

Always do up your seat belt before a journey.

sew (verb)

To sew means to join pieces of cloth together with thread. You use a sharp needle to sew.

When I sew, I make a row of little stitches.

shadow (noun)
A shadow is a dark area that appears behind an object when light shines on it.

When the sun shines on my face, my shadow is behind me.

shake (verb)
To shake means to move something backwards and forwards, or from side to side.

I shake the bottle to make the sauce come out.

shallow (adjective)
Shallow means not very deep.

The cat sat in a shallow puddle.

shampoo (noun)
Shampoo is a liquid soap that you use to wash your hair.

Shampoo is bubbly when you rub it on your hair.

share (verb)
To share means to give part of something to others.

Julia shares her cake with her best friend.

shark (noun)
A shark is a big fish that lives in the sea. Most have a fin on their back and lots of sharp teeth.

Some sharks hunt fish and other animals to eat.

shed (noun)
A shed is a small building, usually made of wood, that is used for storing things.

The shed in the garden is full of tools.

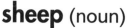

sheep (noun)
A sheep is a farm animal with a thick, woolly coat. A baby sheep is called a lamb.

Sheep live outside in grassy fields.

shell (noun)

A shell is a hard covering on the outside of something. Eggs, nuts and some animals have shells.

We found an empty shell on the beach.

shiver (verb)

To shiver is to shake all over. You might shiver when you feel cold, ill or frightened.

The cold water made her shiver.

shine (verb)

To shine means to give out light.

When I shine my torch I can read in the dark.

shoe (noun)

A shoe is something that you wear on each foot to keep you comfortable, warm and dry.

Put on a pair of shoes before you go outside.

ship (noun)

A ship is a large boat. It can carry people or objects across the water.

The ship sails out of the harbour.

shop (noun)

A shop is a place where you buy things.

The toy shop sells lots of games and toys.

shirt (noun)

A shirt is something you wear on the top part of your body. It can have long or short sleeves.

My shirt has orange buttons down the front.

short (adjective)

Something that is short is not very long, or very tall.

My brother is short, but my sister is tall.

93

shoulder (noun)
Your shoulder is the place where your arm joins onto your body. You have two shoulders.

I can touch my shoulders.

sing (verb)
To sing means to make musical sounds with your voice.

My cousin loves to sing pop songs!

shout (verb)
To shout means to speak or call out very loudly.

I get told off when I shout at my brother.

sink (noun)
A sink is a bowl that is fixed to the wall in a kitchen or bathroom. You fill a sink with water from the taps.

Put the washing-up in the kitchen sink!

shower (noun)
A shower is an object which sprays water. You stand underneath to wash yourself.

The water in the shower feels nice and warm.

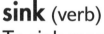

sink (verb)
To sink means to move downwards. When you throw a pebble into water, it sinks to the bottom.

In the evening, the sun sinks lower in the sky.

shut (adjective)
When something is shut, it is closed. Shut is the opposite of open.

Make sure the door is shut when you leave the house!

sister (noun)
Your sister is a girl, or a woman, with the same parents as you.

My sister can play the drums.

94

a b c d e f g h i j k l m n o p q r s t u v w x y z

skate (verb)

To skate means to glide across a smooth surface. You usually wear special boots to skate.

I wear ice skates to skate at the ice rink.

skip (verb)

To skip means to jump or hop over something, or to spring from one foot to the other.

I can skip with my skipping rope.

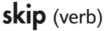

skateboard (noun)

A skateboard is a short board with four wheels underneath. You stand on a skateboard to ride along.

My skateboard is orange.

skirt (noun)

A skirt is a piece of clothing that fits around the waist and hangs down over the legs.

My cousin is wearing a spotty skirt.

skeleton (noun)

A skeleton is all the bones that make a person's or animal's body.

There are more than 200 bones in your skeleton.

skull (noun)

A skull is a set of bones that make a person's or animal's head. Your skull protects your brain.

A pirate flag has a picture of a skull on it.

ski (noun)

A ski is a long, thin piece of wood or plastic that you wear on each foot to glide over snow or water.

Snow skis clip to special ski boots.

sky (noun)

The sky is the space you see above you when you are outside. It is blue or grey in the day and black at night.

The night sky is full of stars.

a b c d e f g h i j k l m n o p q r s t u v w x y z

skyscraper (noun)

A skyscraper is a very tall building. Most skyscrapers are built in the middle of big cities.

These skyscrapers are taller than the trees!

sleeve (noun)

A sleeve is the part of a coat or shirt that covers your arm.

My shirt has long sleeves.

sledge (noun)

A sledge is something you ride on to slide down a snowy slope. It is made of wood or plastic.

I sit on my sledge and speed down the hill!

slice (noun)

A slice is a thin piece of something. A slice is cut from a bigger piece.

Dad cut a slice of bread.

sleep (verb)

When you sleep you close your eyes and rest. You don't know what is going on around you.

Our dog likes to sleep on his blanket.

slide (noun)

A slide is something you play on. It has a ladder up to a long, smooth slope which you slide down.

I like the big slide in the playground.

sleeping bag (noun)

A sleeping bag is a warm cover that you sleep in. You climb inside and zip it up.

I sleep in a sleeping bag when I go camping.

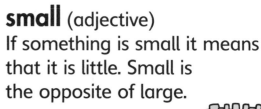

small (adjective)

If something is small it means that it is little. Small is the opposite of large.

I had a small bag of chips and my parents had a large bag of chips.

smell (verb)
To smell means to notice a scent by breathing through your nose.

I can smell the toast burning!

snail (noun)
A snail is a small creature with a soft body and a shell on its back.

A snail can hide inside its shell.

smile (verb)
To smile means to turn up the corners of your mouth when you feel happy.

Smile for the photograph!

snake (noun)
A snake is an animal with a long, thin body and no legs. It moves by slithering along the ground.

The snake has brightly coloured skin.

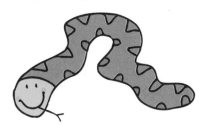

smooth (adjective)
Something is smooth if it has no bumps or lumps in it, or on it.

Smooth ice is fun to skate on.

sneeze (verb)
When you sneeze, air suddenly comes out of your mouth and nose. A sneeze makes a noise that sounds like "A-tishoo!"

When I smell pepper it makes me sneeze!

snack (noun)
A snack is a small amount of food that you eat between meals.

An apple makes a tasty snack.

sniff (verb)
To sniff means to breathe in quickly through your nose.
The dog sniffs the ground to find his buried bone.

snorkel (noun)
A snorkel is a tube that you put in your mouth so that you can breathe if your face is underwater.

I use a snorkel and a mask to swim in the sea.

sock (noun)
A sock is a piece of clothing, made from soft cloth, that you wear on each foot.

I have a pair of stripy socks.

snow (noun)
Snow is soft, white flakes of ice that fall from the sky. Snow falls when it is very cold.

The trees are covered in thick snow.

sofa (noun)
A sofa is a long, comfortable seat. Two or three people can sit on a sofa together.

This sofa has cushions on it.

snowman (noun)
A snowman is a model of a person made from snow.

This snowman has a carrot for a nose.

soft (adjective)
When something is soft, it is easy to squeeze and feels nice to touch. Soft is the opposite of hard.

My teddy bear is soft and cuddly.

soap (noun)
Soap is something that is used to wash your body. You mix it with water and rub it to make bubbles.

This bar of soap smells nice.

soil (noun)
Soil is another word for the earth on the ground. Plants grow in soil.

The gardener digs the soil with a spade.

sole (noun)
Your sole is the bottom of your foot or shoe. It is the part that you stand and walk on.

Is the sole of your foot ticklish?

soup (noun)
Soup is a tasty liquid made from cooked meat, fish or vegetables. You eat soup with a spoon.

Tomato soup is my favourite.

solid (noun)
A solid is something hard or firm that has a shape. It is the opposite of a liquid.

Ice is water that has frozen solid.

space (noun)
Space is the huge area far above the Earth where there are stars, moons and planets.

At night, you can see the Moon in space.

somersault (verb)
To somersault means to roll all the way over – head over heels.

I can somersault forwards and backwards.

spaceship (noun)
A spaceship is a vehicle that takes people into space.

A spaceship has big engines to lift it off the ground.

sore (adjective)
Sore means painful. When something is sore, it hurts.

My knee felt sore when I cut it.

spaghetti (noun)
Spaghetti is a kind of pasta that looks like long pieces of string.

I like spaghetti and meatballs.

a b c d e f g h i j k l m n o p q r s t u v w x y z

sparrow (noun)
A sparrow is a small, brown bird. Sparrows live in the wild.

I fed the sparrow some crumbs.

spend (verb)
When you spend money, you use it to buy things.

I like to spend my money at the toy shop.

speak (verb)
To speak means to say words. You use your mouth to speak.

I speak to my friends on the telephone.

spider (noun)
A spider is a small animal with eight legs. Some spiders make webs to catch flies to eat.

A spider spins a web from threads of silk.

speed (verb)
To speed means to travel very fast. A person who speeds in a car on a normal road is driving too fast.

The racing driver speeds around the racetrack.

spill (verb)
If you spill something, you let it fall out of its container.

The milk will spill if you tip the jug!

spell (verb)
To spell a word means to say or write each letter in the correct order.

You can use a dictionary to help you spell words.

spoon (noun)
A spoon has a long handle and a round end. You eat puddings and runny foods with a spoon.

Spoons are often made of metal.

squirrel (noun)

A squirrel is a small, wild animal with a long, bushy tail.

The squirrel has some acorns to eat.

star (noun)

A star is a bright object that shines in the night sky.

I like to look at the stars at night.

stable (noun)

A stable is a building where a horse is kept.

The horse looked out of his stable.

starfish (noun)

A starfish is a sea creature. It usually has five arms and is shaped like a star.

This starfish is blue.

stadium (noun)

A stadium is a place where people watch sport or music events. It usually has a field with seats around the edge.

The stadium is packed with football fans.

station (noun)

A station is a place where trains or buses pick up and drop off passengers.

You can buy your train ticket at the station.

stair (noun)

A stair is a step that you walk up or down. You climb the stairs to get to rooms at the top of a house.

I climb the stairs at bedtime.

statue (noun)

A statue is a model of a person or an animal. Most statues are made from stone, metal or wood.

A statue stands in the middle of the town.

steam (noun)

Steam is the hot, white cloud of gas that is made when water boils.

Steam comes from the spout of the boiling kettle.

stem (noun)

A stem is the long, thin part of a plant. Leaves and flowers grow on a stem.

You cut the stem when you pick a flower.

stick (noun)

A stick is a long, thin piece of wood. You might find a stick under a tree.

If you throw a stick, our dog will bring it back!

stir (verb)

To stir means to move things around so they mix together.

The cook uses a spoon to stir the stew.

stool (noun)

A stool is a small seat with no back or arms.

Some stools only have three legs.

storm (noun)

A storm is a time of very bad weather, with rain and strong winds.

A storm may bring thunder and lightning.

story (noun)

A story tells you about things that have or could have happened. Stories can be true or made up.

My teacher reads a story to the class every day.

straight (adjective)

When something is straight, it has no curves or bends in it.

You use a ruler to draw a straight line.

a b c d e f g h i j k l m n o p q r s t u v w x y z

strawberry (noun)

A strawberry is a soft, red fruit that grows near the ground. It is sweet to eat.

A strawberry has little seeds on the outside.

strong (adjective)

If something is strong, it is hard to break, or it is able to lift or move heavy things.

A horse is strong enough to pull a cart.

street (noun)

A street is a road in a city or town. A street often has buildings on each side.

There are lots of shops along this street.

submarine (noun)

A submarine is a ship that can travel underwater.

A submarine can dive down very deep.

string (noun)

String is long, thin rope that you use to tie things together.

The balloons are tied to pieces of string.

suitcase (noun)

A suitcase is a big bag with strong sides and a handle. It is used to carry clothes when you travel.

Have you packed your suitcase for the holiday?

stripe (noun)

A stripe is a line of colour.

This scarf has green stripes on it.

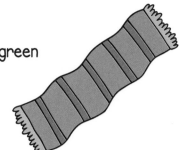

sum (noun)

A sum is a simple maths question, such as when you add two numbers together.

The answer to the sum $3 + 6$ is 9.

a b c d e f g h i j k l m n o p q r s t u v w x y z

sun (noun)
The sun shines in the sky in the daytime. It is the star that warms the Earth and gives us light.

The sun is very hot in summer.

surf (verb)
When you surf, you ride a wave on the sea. You stand or lie on a special board to surf.

I can surf really big waves.

sunflower (noun)
A sunflower is a tall plant, usually with one big, yellow flower.

The centre of a sunflower is full of seeds.

surprise (noun)
A surprise is something that you do not expect to happen.

My friend has a big surprise for me!

sunglasses (noun)
Sunglasses are dark glasses that you wear to protect your eyes from bright sunshine.

I wear my sunglasses on a sunny day.

swan (noun)
A swan is a large bird with a long neck that lives on rivers and lakes. A swan is usually white.

The swan paddles through the water.

supermarket (noun)
A supermarket is a large shop that sells food, and other things for the home.

We put our shopping in a trolley at the supermarket.

swimming pool (noun)
A swimming pool is a large tank that is filled with water where people can swim.

You climb down the ladder to get into the swimming pool.

104

Tt

table (noun)

A table has a flat top and four legs. You can sit at a table to eat your meals.

Can you lay the table for dinner?

tale (noun)

A tale is a story that is usually made up.

My favourite fairy tale is *Cinderella*.

tadpole (noun)

A tadpole is a baby frog. When it hatches from its egg, it has a large head and a long, wriggly tail.

The tadpole will grow legs as it gets older.

talk (verb)

To talk means to say words. When you talk, you speak to another person.

My sister talks to her friends for hours!

tail (noun)

A tail is the part of an animal's body that sticks out at the bottom of its back.

A dog wags its tail when it is happy.

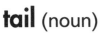

tall (adjective)

When something is tall, it is very high. Tall is the opposite of short.

There is a tall tower in the middle of the city.

tambourine (noun)

A tambourine is a round musical instrument with small, metal circles around the edge.

When I shake the tambourine it makes a jingling sound.

taxi (noun)

A taxi is a car with a driver. You pay the driver to take you where you want to go.

I took a taxi to the airport.

tape measure (noun)

A tape measure is a long, thin strip of cloth or metal with numbers marked on it. It is used to measure things.

This tape measure slides in and out of its case.

tea (noun)

Tea is a drink made by pouring boiling water onto dried leaves from a tea plant.

My mum drinks tea at breakfast time.

target (noun)

A target is something that you try to hit. It is usually a circle with a pattern of coloured rings on it.

He hit the middle of the target with his arrow.

teach (verb)

To teach means to tell, or show, someone how to do something.

Can you teach me how to play the violin?

taste (verb)

To taste means to try food or drink to find out what flavour it is. You taste with your tongue.

She wants to taste the cheese before she buys it.

teacher (noun)

A teacher is a person whose job it is to teach others. Most teachers work in a school.

My teacher rings a bell at the end of playtime.

tear (noun)

A tear is a drop of salty liquid that comes from your eye.

Tears run down my cheeks when I cry.

tear (verb)

To tear means to pull something apart. If you tear something in half you will have two pieces.

Be careful not to tear the pages!

teddy bear (noun)

A teddy bear is a furry toy. Teddy bears can be small or large, and they are very cuddly.

My teddy bear sleeps in my bed at night.

teenager (noun)

A teenager is a young person who is between 13 and 19 years old.

My brother and his friends are teenagers.

telephone (noun)

A telephone is a machine that lets you talk to someone in another place. It is also called a phone.

You answer the telephone when it rings.

telescope (noun)

A telescope is something which makes things that are far away look closer.

You can see far-off planets when you look through a telescope.

television (noun)

A television is a machine with a screen that shows moving pictures and sounds.

I like to watch pop stars on the television.

tell (verb)

To tell means to say something to another person.
My grandpa tells me stories at bedtime.

a
b
c
d
e
f
g
h
i
j
k
l
m
n
o
p
q
r
s
t
u
v
w
x
y
z

tennis (noun)
Tennis is a sport played on a court by two or four people. You have to hit a ball over a net with a racket.

I play tennis with my friends.

thermometer (noun)
A thermometer is an object that tells you how hot or cold something is.

A nurse uses a thermometer to find out if a person is too hot.

tent (noun)
A tent is an outdoor shelter made of strong fabric. You can fold up a tent and carry it with you.

We sleep in a tent when we go camping.

thick (adjective)
If something is thick it is fat or wide. Thick is the opposite of thin.

A thick book has a lot of pages.

test (noun)
A test is a set of questions to answer. When you do a test it shows how much you know.

My teacher gives us a spelling test every Monday.

thigh (noun)
Your thigh is the top part of your leg. It is between your knee and your hip.

Her thighs hurt after climbing the mountain.

theatre (noun)
A theatre is a place with a stage and rows of seats. You watch a play or a show at the theatre.

We had seats in the front row of the theatre.

thin (adjective)
Something that is thin is very narrow. Something thin is not thick or fat.

The monster has long, thin arms and legs.

thirsty (adjective)

If you are thirsty, you feel like you want a drink.

He felt thirsty after a long, hot walk.

throne (noun)

A throne is a special chair for a king or a queen. A throne is usually used for an important event.

The cat sat on the golden throne.

thistle (noun)

A thistle is a type of plant with prickly leaves and a colourful flower.

Thistles often grow in wild places.

throw (verb)

When you throw something you make it fly through the air by moving your arm forwards and letting go.

I throw the ball to my sister.

thorn (noun)

A thorn is a sharp point that grows on some plants.

Be careful of rose thorns!

thumb (noun)

A thumb is the short, thick part on each hand. Thumbs makes it easy to pick up and hold onto things.

I stick up my thumbs to show that I like something.

thread (noun)

A thread is a long, thin piece of material. Thread is used to sew things together.

I used blue thread to do some sewing.

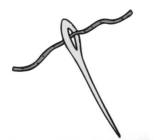

thunder (noun)

Thunder is a very loud rumble in the sky. You hear thunder when there is a storm.

I heard thunder and then it started raining.

a b c d e f g h i j k l m n o p q r s t u v w x y z

ticket (noun)

A ticket is a piece of paper that shows that you have paid to travel somewhere, or to see or do something.

How much is a ticket for the show?

tiger (noun)

A tiger is a large, wild animal. It is a big cat with orange fur and black stripes.

A tiger is a strong and fierce animal.

tide (noun)

The tide is the rise and fall of the sea. Water moves up the beach when the tide comes in.

When the tide goes out, I can walk across the sand.

tight (adjective)

If something is tight, it fits very closely.

My coat is so tight that I can't do it up.

tie (noun)

A tie is a long, thin piece of material worn in a special knot under a shirt collar.

His tie has red and purple stripes.

tiptoe (verb)

To tiptoe means to walk very quietly on your toes.

I tiptoe past the baby's room when she is sleeping.

tie (verb)

If you tie something you fasten two ends together with a knot or a bow.

The sailor ties a knot in the rope.

toad (noun)

A toad is an an animal that looks like a frog. Most toads live on land and move by making small hops.

A toad has dry, bumpy skin.

toadstool (noun)

A toadstool is a kind of mushroom with a round top. Toadstools can be poisonous.

We found a red, spotty toadstool in the wood.

tomato (noun)

A tomato is a round, red fruit with lots of seeds inside. Tomatoes can be eaten cooked or uncooked.

I like lots of tomatoes in my salad.

toast (noun)

Toast is a slice of bread that has been heated until it is crisp on the outside.

The toast popped out of the toaster.

tongue (noun)

Your tongue is the soft, pink part that you can move inside your mouth. You use it to taste and to talk.

It is rude to stick out your tongue!

toddler (noun)

A toddler is a young child who has just learned to walk.

A toddler can walk without help from a grown-up.

tool (noun)

A tool is an object that helps you to do a job. Hammers, saws and screwdrivers are tools.

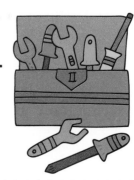

My dad keeps his tools in a toolbox.

toe (noun)

A toe is one of the five parts at the end of each foot. Your toes are all different sizes.

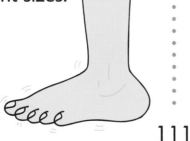

Can you wiggle your toes?

tooth (noun)

A tooth is one of the many hard, white objects inside your mouth. It is used for biting or chewing.

My front tooth fell out today!

111

a b c d e f g h i j k l m n o p q r s **t** u v w x y z

toothbrush (noun)

A toothbrush is used for cleaning teeth. It has a small brush at one end and a thin handle.

My toothbrush is red and my toothpaste is stripy.

toucan (noun)

A toucan is a bird that lives in the jungle. It has a large, colourful beak.

How many colours can you see on this toucan's beak?

torch (noun)

A torch is a small light that you hold in your hand. A torch has batteries to make it work.

I switch on my torch to see in the dark.

towel (noun)

A towel is a soft cloth that you use to dry yourself when you are wet.

This beach towel has pictures of fish on it.

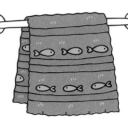

tornado (noun)

A tornado is a very strong wind. It spins round and round in circles as it moves across the ground.

A tornado can rip up trees and houses.

tower (noun)

A tower is a tall, thin building. You can see a tower from far away because it is so high.

Rapunzel lived at the top of a tower.

tortoise (noun)

A tortoise is an animal with a hard, thick shell on its back. It tucks its head inside its shell when it sleeps.

A tortoise walks very slowly.

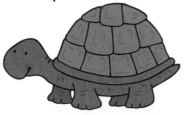

toy (noun)

A toy is something that a child plays with. Teddy bears, building blocks and train sets are all toys.

I keep my toys in a toy box.

tractor (noun)

A tractor is a farm vehicle with big wheels. It pulls heavy loads and machines.

The farmer drives her tractor across the muddy field.

trampoline (noun)

A trampoline is something that you jump up and down on. It has strong springs around the edge to make it bouncy.

I can jump really high on my trampoline.

traffic (noun)

Traffic is what we call all the cars, buses, trucks, bicycles and motorbikes that travel on roads.

There is a lot of traffic in town today.

travel (verb)

To travel means to go from one place to another.

When I go to school, I travel by bus.

trail (noun)

A trail is the smell, footprints or marks left by a person or animal as they move along.

He is following the trail of footprints.

tray (noun)

A tray is a flat piece of wood or plastic. You carry things such as drinks and food on a tray.

There are three milkshakes on the tray.

train (noun)

A train is a vehicle that travels along tracks. It has an engine that pulls coaches full of people or goods.

The train speeds along the tracks.

treasure (noun)

Treasure is gold, money, jewels and other precious things.

The pirates buried a chest full of treasure.

tree (noun)

A tree is a kind of tall plant. It has a wooden trunk and branches. Leaves, nuts and fruit can grow on trees.

This tree has green leaves.

truck (noun)

A truck is a very big vehicle that travels on roads. A truck can carry heavy loads.

The truck is full of rocks.

trick (noun)

A trick is when someone does something clever to entertain people. A magician does magic tricks.

My brother does a funny trick with cards.

trumpet (noun)

A trumpet is a musical instrument. You blow into one end and sounds come out of the other end.

You have to blow hard to play the trumpet.

tricycle (noun)

A tricycle is something you ride on. It has one wheel at the front and two wheels at the back.

I take Teddy for rides on my tricycle.

trunk (noun)

A trunk is an elephant's long nose. Elephants use their trunks to breathe, pick up food and suck up water.

The elephant sprayed water out of her trunk.

trip (noun)

A trip is when you go somewhere and then come back home again.

My family went on a trip to the zoo.

trunk (noun)

A trunk is also the thick, wooden stem of a tree. Branches grow from the trunk.

I tried to put my arms around the tree trunk.

trunk (noun)
A trunk is also a big, strong box with a lid.

We found Grandma's old trunk in the attic.

turtle (noun)
A turtle is a wild animal with a hard shell. Turtles can live in rivers or in the sea.

A mother sea turtle lays her eggs in the sand.

T-shirt (noun)
A T-shirt is a shirt with short sleeves and no collar. T-shirts are often made of soft cotton.

My favourite T-shirt has a sun on it.

tusk (noun)
A tusk is a long, pointed tooth. Elephants and walruses have a tusk on each side of their mouth.

An elephant uses its tusks to dig for food.

tube (noun)
A tube is a long container which is usually made of soft plastic or thin metal.

Toothpaste comes in a tube.

twin (noun)
A twin is a person with a brother or sister who was born on the same day and who has the same parents.

My friends are twins, and they dress the same every day.

turn (verb)
When you turn something you move it around. You can turn something to face the other way.

I turn my head from side to side.

twist (verb)
To twist means to turn something, or to wrap one thing around another.

You twist the lid of a jar to open it.

a b c d e f g h i j k l m n o p q r s t u v w x y z

U u

umbrella (noun)

You hold an umbrella over your head to keep you dry when it rains. You fold it away when the rain stops.

I put up my umbrella when it started to rain.

uniform (noun)

A uniform is a set of clothes that people wear to do a job, or to go to a school, or a club.

Police officers and nurses wear a uniform.

underwear (noun)

Underwear is the clothing that you wear next to your skin. You wear other clothes over your underwear.

Some underwear is brightly coloured.

untidy (adjective)

Untidy means messy, or not neat.

Our toy cupboard is very untidy.

unicorn (noun)

A unicorn is a made-up creature. It looks like a horse with a horn on the front of its head.

You read about unicorns in fairy tales.

upload (verb)

To upload means to send information from one computer or phone to another computer, or the Internet.

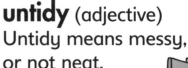

I am going to upload a photo to my computer.

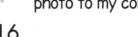

V v

valley (noun)

A valley is the low land between hills or mountains.

This valley has a river running through it.

vase (noun)

A vase is a container for flowers. You fill it with water and place the flower stems inside.

I found a vase to put my tulips in.

vegetable (noun)

A vegetable is part of a plant that you can eat. Potatoes, carrots and peas are vegetables.

Which vegetables do you like to eat?

vehicle (noun)

A vehicle is any machine with wheels that takes people or things from one place to another.

Cars, trains, buses and lorries are vehicles.

vet (noun)

A vet is a doctor who looks after animals. You take your pet to a vet when it is ill.

Our cat does not like going to the vet.

violin (noun)

A violin is a wooden musical instrument with four strings. You play it with a long stick, called a bow.

To play a violin, you hold it under your chin.

a b c d e f g h i j k l m n o p q r s t u v w x y z

Ww

walk (verb)

To walk means to move along by putting one foot in front of the other.

I like to walk in the park with my dog.

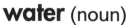

water (noun)

Water is the clear liquid in rivers, lakes and seas. Water also falls out of the sky as rain.

Water for washing and drinking comes from a tap.

warm (adjective)

When you are warm, you feel just right. You are not too hot or too cold.

The sun feels warm on my face.

waterfall (noun)

A waterfall is where water from a river or stream falls from a high place to a lower place.

It is a long way to the bottom of the waterfall.

washing machine (noun)

A washing machine cleans dirty clothes with water and soap.

The clothes in the washing machine spin round and round.

wave (noun)

A wave is a big ripple of water that moves across the sea. When the wind blows it makes waves.

The waves crashed onto the beach.

wave (verb)

To wave is to move your hand from side to side when you say goodbye.

My dad waves to us when he goes to work.

weigh (verb)

You weigh something to find out how heavy it is. You use scales to weigh people and things.

It is hard to weigh an elephant!

weather (noun)

The weather is what it is like outside. Rain, wind and snow are kinds of weather.

I don't like wet weather because I have to stay inside.

whale (noun)

A whale is a huge sea animal. A whale breathes through a hole on the top of its head.

The blue whale is the biggest animal in the world.

website (noun)

A website is a set of pages that you find on the Internet. Schools and businesses have websites.

You can look at a website on a computer or a phone.

wheel (noun)

A wheel is a round object that turns. Vehicles such as cars and buses move along on wheels.

A tractor has big wheels, but a scooter has small wheels.

week (noun)

Every week has seven days in it. There are 52 weeks in one year.

Do you know the names of the days of the week?

wheelchair (noun)

A wheelchair is a seat with wheels. People who cannot walk use a wheelchair to get around.

My wheelchair has soft blue arms.

a b c d e f g h i j k l m n o p q r s t u v **w** x y z

whisker (noun)

A whisker is one of the long hairs that grow on the face of a cat, mouse or other animal.

My cat has short whiskers.

witch (noun)

A witch is a woman who does magic. You read about witches in made-up stories.

The witch has a black cat.

whistle (noun)

A whistle is a small object that makes a sound. You put it to your lips and blow into it.

The whistle makes a loud, high sound.

wizard (noun)

A wizard is a man who has magical powers. You read about wizards in made-up stories.

I like to dress up as a wizard.

wild (adjective)

If something is wild it is not looked after by people. Animals and plants can be wild.

Zebras and giraffes are wild animals.

woman (noun)

A woman is a grown-up girl.

My doctor is a woman and so is my teacher.

window (noun)

A window is an opening in a wall or vehicle that is usually filled with glass. It lets in air and light.

What can you see out of the window?

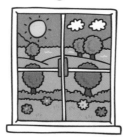

wood (noun)

Wood is the hard material in the trunk and branches of a tree. We use wood to build and make things.

The table and chair are made of wood.

wool (noun)

Wool is the soft thread that is made from a sheep's thick hair. Warm clothes are made from wool.

My grandma used yellow wool to knit me a jumper.

write (verb)

When you write, you put words or numbers onto paper with a pen or pencil, or type them on a computer or phone.

She writes in her diary every day.

word (noun)

A word is a sound that has a meaning. You can say, read or write words.

This book has lots of words in it.

wrong (adjective)

Wrong is not right. A wrong answer is not the correct one.

Is this answer right or wrong?

Xx

x-ray (noun)

An x-ray is a special photograph. It lets a doctor see inside your body. X-rays are taken at a hospital.

The x-ray shows the bones in her arm.

xylophone (noun)

A xylophone is a musical instrument. It has rows of flat, wooden bars that you hit with small hammers.

Can you play a tune on a xylophone?

121

a b c d e f g h i j k l m n o p q r s t u v w x y z

Yy

yawn (verb)
You open your mouth wide when you yawn. People yawn when they are tired or bored.

I yawn when I am ready to go to bed.

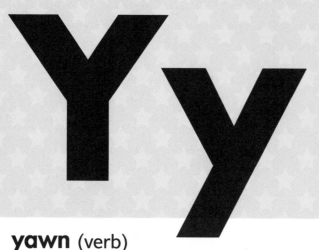

year (noun)
A year is 12 months, or 52 weeks, long. There are four seasons in a year.

You have a birthday every year.

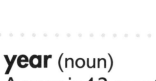

yell (verb)
To yell means to shout out loudly.

I yell to my friends when I see them across the street.

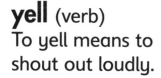

yoghurt (noun)
Yoghurt is a sour food that is made from milk. Sugar and fruit can be added to yoghurt.

Cherry yoghurt is pink and tastes sweet.

yolk (noun)
The yolk is the yellow part in the middle of an egg.

Which part of an egg do you like best - the yolk or the white?

young (adjective)
You are young if you were born a short time ago. Young means not old.

My little sister is very young.

122

Zz

zebra (noun)

A zebra is a wild animal that looks like a horse. It has black and white stripes.

Zebras live in Africa.

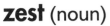

zest (noun)

Zest is the name for the thin layer of skin on the outside of an orange, lemon or lime.

You can use lemon zest to add flavour to food.

zigzag (noun)

A zigzag is a spiky line that goes up and down, or forwards and backwards.

You can draw a zigzag by joining lots of Vs together.

zip (noun)

A zip is used to fasten openings on clothes or bags. It has rows of tiny teeth that slot together when you slide the tab.

The zip on my coat is easy to do up.

zoo (noun)

A zoo is a place where wild animals are kept. People visit a zoo to see the animals.

We watched the seals and the penguins at the zoo.

zoom (verb)

Something zooms when it moves very fast.

My toy car zooms along the floor.

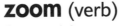

Colours

Read the descriptions below. The colour words are adjectives because they are describing the animal words. The animal words are nouns.

grey cat

blue butterfly

brown monkey

yellow fish

green frog

pink pig

orange tiger

grey elephant

white lamb

Opposites

Some words have opposite meanings. This means they are completely different from each other, like 'wet' and 'dry'.
These are some useful opposites.

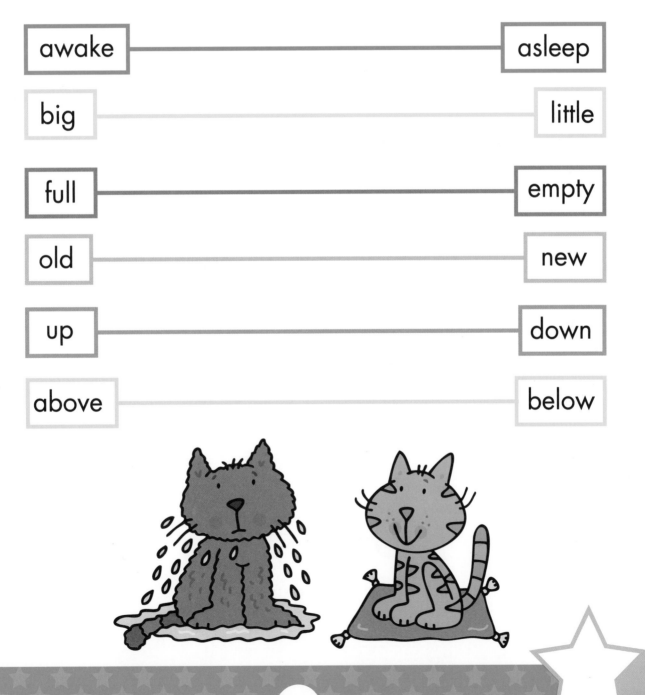

awake	asleep
big	little
full	empty
old	new
up	down
above	below

125

Days, weeks and months

The year is divided into days, weeks and months. There are 7 days in a week and there are 52 weeks in one year. The year is divided into 12 months.

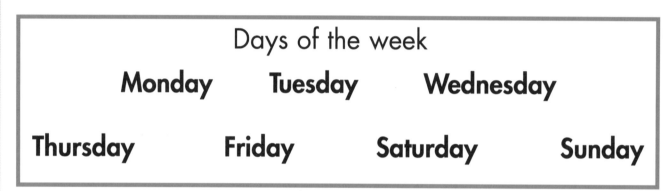

Days of the week

Monday   **Tuesday**   **Wednesday**

Thursday   **Friday**   **Saturday**   **Sunday**

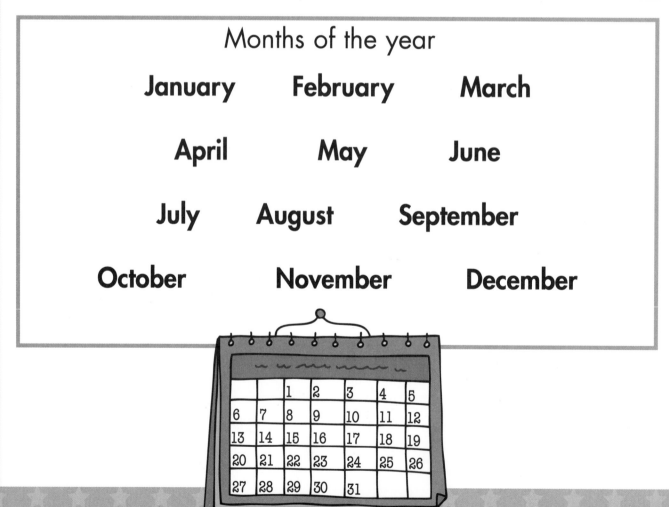

Months of the year

January   **February**   **March**

April   **May**   **June**

July   **August**   **September**

October   **November**   **December**

You can use this poem to help you remember how many days are in each month.

30 days has September, April,
June and November.
All the rest have 31,
Except February alone,
Which has 28 days clear,
And 29 in each leap year.

In some parts of the world, the year can be divided into four seasons. A season changes when the weather changes, and the days get shorter or longer.

spring

summer

autumn

winter

Answers

Page 5

'E' comes before 'F'.

'T' comes after 'S'.

Page 7

Helicopter is a noun.

Sniff is a verb.

Atlas is a noun.

Fall is a verb.

Magazine is a noun.

Sock is a noun.

Cave is a noun.

Write is a verb.

Melon is a noun.